1-97

D0478338

America's Reconstruction

America's Reconstruction

PEOPLE AND POLITICS AFTER THE CIVIL WAR

Eric Foner and Olivia Mahoney

HarperPerennial

A Division of HarperCollins*Publishers*

AMERICA'S RECONSTRUCTION. Copyright © 1995 by Eric Foner and Olivia Mahoney. All rights reserved. Printed in the United States of America. No part of this book may be used or reproduced in any manner whatsoever without written permission except in the case of brief quotations embodied in critical articles and reviews. For information address HarperCollins Publishers, Inc., 10 East 53rd Street, New York, NY 10022.

HarperCollins books may be purchased for educational, business, or sales promotional use. For information please write: Special Markets Department, HarperCollins Publishers, Inc., 10 East 53rd Street, New York, NY 10022.

FIRST EDITION

Designed by Laura Lindgren

Library of Congress Cataloging-in-Publication Data

Foner, Eric.
America's Reconstruction : people and politics after the Civil War
/ Eric Foner and Olivia Mahoney. — 1st ed.
    p. cm.
Includes bibliographical references and index.
ISBN 0-06-055346-4 (cloth) — ISBN 0-06-096989-X (pbk.)
1. Reconstruction. 2. United States—Politics and government—1865–1877.
I. Mahoney, Olivia, 1952– . II. Title.
E668.F65 1995
973.8'1—dc20   94-40387
95 96 97 98 99 ❖/RRD 10 9 8 7 6 5 4 3 2 1

973.81
FON
1995

To my uncles, Henry, Moe, and Philip Foner
And for Vasile Bouleanu

CONTENTS

Color illustrations follow page 80.

FOREWORD

In 1987 the Valentine Museum set out to write the first scholarly history of its city, Richmond, Virginia. A number of scholars helped the museum establish an agenda of research projects that would provide the material necessary for a new synthesis.

Race was identified as an issue at the heart of the city's past and the most important issue in Richmond's present. The museum thus began to develop a series of research projects and exhibitions to begin a public discussion of the topic. In addition to four exhibitions that explored race in the twentieth century, the museum studied the antebellum African-American community and its relationship with white communities in the exhibitions *In Bondage and Freedom: Antebellum Black Life in Richmond* (1988) and *Shared Spaces, Separate Lives* (1993); the Civil War and its impact on the mind of the city in *Why the South Lost the Civil War* (1988); and the period after the nominal end of Reconstruction in *Jim Crow: Racism and Reaction in the New South* (1989).

The period of Reconstruction still existed as a gap in the Valentine's public discussion. The museum was eager therefore to explore, with Eric Foner and Olivia Mahoney, the development of an exhibition on Reconstruction rooted in Foner's influential scholarship, to follow their important exhibition *A House Divided: America in the Age of Lincoln,* which opened at the Chicago Historical Society in 1990. The project offered an opportunity to create a major traveling exhibition that would bring Foner's work to a wider audience.

It is of the greatest importance that this work reach the broadest possible public because the question of race remains at the heart of the life of Richmond and America. Reconstruction is possibly the most misunderstood era in the American past, despite the fact that its scholarly interpretation has undergone enormous changes in the last generation. A distorted view of Reconstruction remains integral to an all-too-easy rationalization for gross injustice and new interpretations of what Foner calls an unfinished revolution that began during the Civil War.

Resolution of this unfinished revolution is central to the life of the Republic. The passage of time has not lifted from us Lincoln's injunction that "It is for us the living, rather, to be dedicated here to the unfinished work which they . . . have thus far so nobly advanced. It is rather for us to be here dedicated to the great task remaining before us . . . that this nation, under God, shall have a new birth of freedom. . . . "

Frank Jewell
Director
Valentine Museum

PREFACE

Reconstruction, one of the most turbulent and controversial eras in American history, began during the Civil War and ended in 1877. It remains relevant today because the issues central to Reconstruction—the role of the federal government in protecting citizens' rights, and the possibility of economic and racial justice in a heterogeneous society—are still unresolved.

Reconstruction witnessed far-reaching changes in America's political and social life. At the national level, new laws and constitutional amendments permanently altered the federal system and the nature of American citizenship. For the first time, the national government assumed the basic responsibility for defining and protecting Americans' civil rights. In the South, African-American men were given the right to vote and hold office—a radical departure from pre–Civil War days, when blacks could vote only in a handful of Northern states. A politically mobilized black community joined with white allies to bring the Republican party to power throughout the South, and with it a redefinition of the purposes and responsibilities of government.

The demise of slavery, the central institution of prewar Southern life, produced profound changes in the social and economic lives of blacks and whites alike. The former slaves sought to breathe full meaning into their newly acquired freedom by establishing their autonomy from white control, including ownership of land. Few white Southerners accepted the idea that African-Americans deserved the same political rights and economic opportunities as themselves, and some sought to reestablish a system of white supremacy as close to slavery as possible. These incompatible definitions of the meaning of freedom produced pervasive conflict in the cities and rural areas of the South. Out of this conflict emerged new systems of labor to replace the shattered world of slavery, and new economic roles for former masters, former slaves, and the white majority that had not owned slaves before the Civil War.

America's Reconstruction: People and Politics After the Civil War is being published in conjunction with a major exhibition on the Reconstruction period that opens at the Valentine Museum in Richmond in 1995 and then will travel to venues in other cities around the country. We believe that this is the first museum exhibition ever devoted exclusively to telling the story of Reconstruction. Including nearly 300 artifacts and images from collections throughout the country, the exhibition examines the origins of Reconstruction during the Civil War; explores how black and white Southerners responded to the Confederacy's defeat and the destruction of slavery; traces the political debate between Congress and President Andrew Johnson that led to the establishment of new Southern governments in which blacks participated; and examines the policies of the Reconstruction governments and the reasons for their overthrow. The exhibition also highlights many of the individuals who shaped the era's history, from Laura Towne, who came to the South Carolina Sea Islands during the Civil War to teach the former slaves, to African-Americans who held public office in the Reconstruction South.

For those who attend the exhibition, we hope this book deepens and prolongs the intellectual and emotional experience of encountering firsthand the material culture of a critical moment in the American past. For other readers, the book stands independently as a short account of Reconstruction, illustrated by well over one hundred of the exhibition's most striking visual images.

No period of our past has undergone in recent years a more complete transformation in historical interpretation than Reconstruction. For much of this century, both scholarly and popular writing presented Reconstruction as an era of unrelieved sordidness in political and social life. According to this view, Abraham Lincoln, before his death, had embarked on a course of sectional reconciliation, which was continued by his successor, Andrew Johnson. Their magnanimous efforts were thwarted by vindictive Radical Republicans in Congress, who fastened black supremacy upon the defeated Confederacy. An orgy of corruption and misgovernment followed, presided over by unscrupulous carpetbaggers (Northerners who ventured South to reap the spoils of office), scalawags, (Southern whites who cooperated with the Republican party for personal gain), and ignorant and childlike freedpeople who were incapable of responsibly exercising the political power that had been thrust upon them. After much needless suffering, the South's white community banded together in patriotic organizations like the Ku Klux Klan to overthrow these "black" governments and restore "home rule" (their euphemism for white supremacy).

Originating in the political propaganda of Reconstruction's opponents, and popularized through films like *Birth of a Nation* (which had its premiere at the White House during Woodrow Wilson's presidency), this interpretation rested on the assumption that black suffrage was the gravest error of the Civil War period. It helped to justify the South's system, which survived into the 1960s, of racial segregation and denying the vote to blacks, as well as the North's acquiescence in Southern nullification of the Fourteenth and Fifteenth Amendments.

Although significant criticisms of the traditional interpretation were advanced earlier in this century, most notably by W. E. B. DuBois in his monumental *Black Reconstruction in America,* published in 1935, it was not until the 1960s that the older view was finally interred. The "Second Reconstruction"—the civil rights movement—inspired among historians a new conception of the first, and in rapid succession virtually every assumption of the old viewpoint was swept away.

In the new scholarship, Andrew Johnson, yesterday's high-minded defender of constitutional principles, was revealed as a racist politician too stubborn to compromise with his critics. Commitment to racial equality, not vindictiveness or mere partisanship, motivated his Radical Republican critics. The period of Radical Reconstruction in the South was shown to be a time of progress for African-Americans and the region as a whole. The Ku Klux Klan, whose campaign of violence had been minimized or excused by earlier historians, was revealed as a terrorist organization that beat and killed its opponents in order to deprive blacks of their newly won rights. Most strikingly, perhaps, African-Americans were now shown to be active agents in shaping the era's history, rather than passive recipients of the actions of others, or simply a "problem" confronting white society.

Today, the Second Reconstruction is over, but the process of historical reinterpretation it unleashed continues apace. Each year, new books and articles on Reconstruction appear. Modern scholars differ among themselves on many issues, but all agree that the traditional view of the period is dead, and unlamented. *America's Reconstruction* draws on the fruits of the past generation of historical writing to present an up-to-date portrait of a period whose unrealized goals still confront our society.

Fugitive Slaves Crossing the Rappahannock River in Virginia,
Timothy H. O'Sullivan, 1862. (Library of Congress)

Even before Abraham Lincoln issued the Emancipation Proclamation in January 1863, thousands of enslaved African-Americans fled to freedom behind the lines of the Union Army as it advanced into Confederate territory. In 1862, Union Army General Benjamin F. Butler designated three escaped slaves as "contrabands of war," or property of military value subject to confiscation. Northern newspapers picked up the term and thereafter slaves who came into Union lines were known as contrabands.

Before Appomattox: Rehearsal for Reconstruction

Reconstruction began not with the Confederacy's surrender in 1865, but during the Civil War. Long before the conflict ended, Americans were debating the questions that came to form the essence of Reconstruction: On what terms should the Southern states be reunited with the Union? Who should establish these terms, Congress or the president? What system of labor should replace plantation slavery? What should be the place of blacks in the political and social life of the South and the nation? None of these questions were settled before 1865, but one definitive conclusion emerged from the Civil War: the reconstructed South would be a society without slavery.

The destruction of slavery powerfully shaped the course of the war and the debate over Reconstruction. Although the Lincoln administration at first insisted that the preservation of the Union was the Civil War's sole object, slaves quickly seized the opportunity to strike for their freedom. As the Union Army occupied Southern territory, first in Virginia, then in Tennessee, Louisiana, and elsewhere, slaves by the thousands headed for the Union lines. A Virginia coachman, informed by soldiers in 1862 that he was free, "went straight to his master's chamber, dressed himself in his best clothes, . . . and insolently informed him that he might for the future drive his own coach." Even in the heart of the Confederacy, the drain of white men into military service left many plantations under the control of planters' wives and elderly and infirm men, whose authority slaves increasingly felt able to challenge. Reports of "insubordinate" activity multiplied throughout the South.

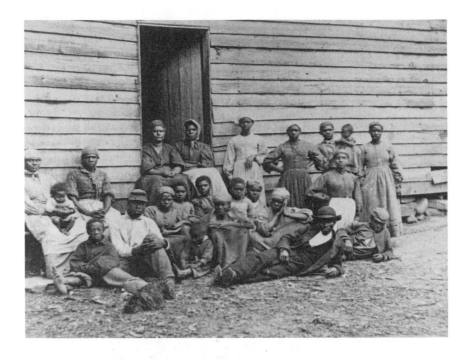

**Contrabands at Follies Farm, Cumberland Landing, Pamunkey River, Virginia,
James F. Gibson, May 1862. (Library of Congress)**

*African-Americans seeking freedom behind Union Army lines included families with young children.
Note the women with traditional African-style headwraps. A boy (lower left) and a young man (on
the right) wear military clothing supplied by the Union Army.*

The disintegration of slavery was one among several considerations that pro-
pelled the Lincoln administration down the road to emancipation. By 1862, lack
of military success, coupled with the antislavery agitation of abolitionists and
Radical Republicans, convinced a significant part of the Northern public that
the war could not be won without attacking slavery. In addition, transforming
the conflict from a struggle to preserve the Union to a crusade against slavery
would, Lincoln believed, forestall the threat that Britain and France might recognize the Confederacy.

Issued on January 1, 1863, Lincoln's Emancipation Proclamation did not
immediately abolish slavery. It applied only to areas of the Confederacy outside
Union control. Excluded from its purview were slaves in Delaware, Maryland,
Kentucky, and Missouri (slave states that had remained within the Union), in

Forever Free, *Mary Edmonia Lewis, marble, 1867.*
(Howard University Gallery of Art, Permanent Collection, Washington, D.C.)

Sculpted to commemorate the ratification of the Thirteenth Amendment, which abolished slavery in the United States, the idealized figures of Forever Free *convey a message of triumph over adversity and hope for the future. Artist Mary Edmonia Lewis, the daughter of a Chippewa Indian mother and an African-American father, created the tableau while studying classical art in Rome; she originally entitled her work* The Morning of Liberty.

Tintypes of black Union soldiers, c. 1864. (Chicago Historical Society)

These photographs of a black sergeant (seated) *and an infantryman* (standing with an officer's sword) *portray two of the nearly 180,000 black Americans who served with the Union Army during the Civil War. A large majority were former slaves. Nearly 40,000 African-Americans lost their lives in the war.*

Army of the James Medal, bronze, 1866.
(National Museum of American History, Smithsonian Institution)

Commissioned by Gen. Benjamin F. Butler, an early proponent of using black combatants, this medal honored black Union troops who seized the summit at the Battle of New Market Heights, Virginia, on September 29, 1864. The medal portrays two black soldiers under a Latin inscription "Freedom Comes Through the Sword."

Albuquerque Academy
Library
6400 Wyoming Blvd. N.E.
Albuquerque, N.M. 87109

Battery A, 2nd U.S. Colored Artillery, Army of the Cumberland, c. 1863.
(Chicago Historical Society)

Members of the 2nd U.S. Colored Artillery posed for this photograph while drilling with a 12-pound Napoleon howitzer, the primary artillery weapon of the Union Army. Black soldiers formed the load team while a white corporal, standing behind the cannon, served as the gunner and aimed the weapon. Black soldiers used the same weapons and received similar training as white soldiers, but they always served in segregated units under white officers.

Tennessee, and in portions of Louisiana and Virginia under federal control. Nonetheless, by decreeing the freedom of the bulk of the nation's black population, well over 3 million men, women, and children, the proclamation sounded the death knell of slavery throughout the country, and profoundly changed the character of the Civil War. Transforming a war of armies into a conflict of societies, it ensured that Union victory would produce a social revolution within the South.

Of the proclamation's provisions, few were more radical in their implications or more essential to breathing life into the promise of emancipation than the enrollment of blacks into military service. Before the war, African-Americans had been excluded from the regular army and militia. In 1861 and 1862, the Lincoln administration had rejected black volunteers, fearing that white soldiers would refuse to serve alongside them. But as the war dragged on and casualties mounted, it became clear that black manpower could not be ignored.

With the proclamation, the enlistment of blacks began in earnest. By the war's end, some 200,000 African-Americans had served in the Union Army and Navy, the large majority of them former slaves. Within the army, black soldiers

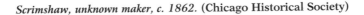

Scrimshaw, unknown maker, c. 1862. (Chicago Historical Society)

When President Lincoln authorized the recruitment of blacks into the military, the Union Army began enlistment drives in occupied territories, including the coastal areas of the Carolinas captured in November 1861. The presence of blacks in the Union Army inspired an unknown maker to inscribe the image of a black soldier on a whale's tooth.

were anything but equal to white. Organized into segregated regiments, they initially received less pay than whites and were assigned largely to fatigue duty and menial labor. Even after proving themselves in battle, they could not advance to the rank of commissioned officer until the very end of the war.

Nonetheless, black soldiers played a crucial role not only in winning the Civil War, but in defining the war's consequences. In the army, African-Americans staked a claim to citizenship. The "logical result" of their military service, one Senator observed in 1864, was that "the black man is henceforth to assume a new status among us." For the first time in American history, large numbers of blacks were treated as equals before the law, if only military law, and the issue of unequal pay sparked a movement among black soldiers that familiarized them with the process of petition and protest and won a signal victory when Congress retroactively accorded them the same compensation as whites. The army was a major source of postwar black political leadership—from its ranks would come many of the black Congressmen, legislators, and other officials of Reconstruction. In time, the black contribution to the Union victory would fade from national memory, but it remained alive within the black community. Growing up in the 1920s, black writer Pauli Murray was "never allowed to forget" that she walked in "proud shoes," because her grandfather, Robert G. Fitzgerald, had "fought for freedom" in the Union Army.

If the Emancipation Proclamation transformed the nature of the Civil War, it also altered the problem of Reconstruction, for the demise of slavery implied far-reaching changes in the South's economy, race relations, and politics. No longer could the Lincoln administration speak of restoring the old Union, or allowing the South to return with its prewar institutions and leadership intact.

Nearly a year elapsed, however, between the proclamation and Lincoln's first announcement of a comprehensive program for Reconstruction. In December 1863, the president offered a pardon to all supporters of the Confederacy, except high-ranking officials, who took an oath of loyalty and pledged to accept the end of slavery. When 10 percent of a state's prewar voters took the oath, they could establish a state government and apply for readmission to the Union. Lincoln decreed that new state constitutions must prohibit slavery, but otherwise gave Southern leaders a free hand in legislation. Voting and office-holding were limited to whites; Lincoln's plan offered the former slaves no role in shaping the South's political future. The 10 Percent Plan, complained abolitionist Wendell Phillips, "frees the slave and ignores the Negro."

Clearly, Lincoln did not believe Reconstruction must involve social and political changes beyond the abolition of slavery. He seems to have assumed that many Southern whites, especially former members of the Whig party (to which he himself had belonged before the slavery issue destroyed it in the 1850s), had been reluctant secessionists and would step forward to accept his lenient terms. It would be a mistake, however, to see the 10 Percent Plan as a hard-and-fast blueprint for the postwar South. Lincoln's Reconstruction policy aimed first and foremost at hastening Union victory and solidifying white support for emancipation. If even a few states chose to accept his plan, this would be a severe blow to the Confederacy.

In 1864, Lincoln attempted to implement his Reconstruction plan. His attention was focused on Louisiana, where Union troops, in 1862, had occupied New Orleans and the surrounding parishes with their large sugar plantations. In

1864, elections were held for a constitutional convention, which abolished slavery and sought Louisiana's readmission to the Union. At the same time, the free blacks of New Orleans—a self-conscious community that included many highly educated, economically successful individuals—pressed for the right to participate in Reconstruction. After meeting with two free black representatives, in March 1864 Lincoln privately, and unsuccessfully, urged Louisiana's governor to allow at least some blacks to vote.

As Reconstruction proceeded in Louisiana, it became clear that many Northern Republicans were unhappy with Lincoln's program. Foremost among them were the Radicals, a group that had led the opposition to slavery's expan-

President Abraham Lincoln, *Alexander Gardner, November 1862.*
(Henry Ford Museum & Greenfield Village)

On December 8, 1863, President Lincoln offered a preliminary plan to reunite Confederate states with the Union. Known as the 10 Percent Plan, Lincoln's proposal offered lenient terms of pardon and amnesty to Confederates who swore allegiance to the United States, but it did not give former slaves any citizenship rights. However, a few days before his death on April 15, 1865, Lincoln endorsed the idea of limited black suffrage, singling out former soldiers and those with some education as most deserving the vote.

sion before the Civil War, and had long favored granting equal civil and political rights to free blacks in the North. They now insisted that the federal government had a responsibility to protect the basic rights of the former slaves. By 1864, many Radicals went further, insisting that Reconstruction could not be secure without black suffrage. Their stance combined principle and political advantage. The Radicals believed that without the right to vote, blacks would be vulnerable to domination by their former owners. They also understood that unless blacks voted, the Republican party would find it very difficult to win elections in the postwar South, and the region's old leaders would return to political power. The Radicals never commanded a majority in Congress, but their commitment to equal rights for the former slaves did much to shape the politics of the next few years.

During 1864, the Radicals became convinced that Lincoln's 10 Percent Plan was too lenient to "rebels" and did too little to protect African-Americans' rights. Enough moderate Republicans agreed that in July, Congress passed the Wade-Davis Bill, which proposed to delay the start of Reconstruction until a majority of a state's white males (not just 10 percent) had taken an oath of loyalty. The new state governments formed under the plan were required not only to prohibit slavery, but to guarantee the equality before the law of black Southerners. Black suffrage, which most Republicans did not at this point support, was not mentioned. Not wishing to abandon his own approach, or the government of Louisiana, Lincoln pocket-vetoed the bill (the president can kill a bill passed within ten days of the end of a congressional session simply by not signing it).

Lincoln and the Radicals differed over Reconstruction, but their breach was not irreparable. Early in 1865, they worked together to secure congressional approval of the Thirteenth Amendment, which irrevocably abolished slavery throughout the nation, including in the border states where the Emancipation Proclamation had not applied. Shortly thereafter, Congress passed, and Lincoln signed, a bill creating the Freedmen's Bureau, an agency empowered to protect the legal rights of the former slaves, provide them with education and medical care, oversee labor contracts between emancipated blacks and their employers, and lease land to black families.

As the act establishing the Freedmen's Bureau suggested, there was far more to Reconstruction than the problem of forming new state governments and determining who should vote. The transition from slavery to freedom posed difficult challenges for national policymakers and involved wrenching changes for both former masters and former slaves, as both sought to define their place in

Copy of the Joint Resolution of the Thirty-eighth Congress . . . Proposing An Amendment to the Constitution . . . Abolishing Slavery, *engraving, D. R. Clark, Western Bank Note and Engraving Co., Chicago, 1868.* (Chicago Historical Society)

In January 1865, the U.S. Congress approved the Thirteenth Amendment to the Constitution, irrevocably abolishing slavery throughout the nation. To commemorate the occasion, members of the House and Senate, along with Speaker of the House Schuyler Colfax, Vice President Hannibal Hamlin, and President Abraham Lincoln signed several copies of the document. For the next several years, commercial printers sold souvenir copies of the historic document.

African-Americans going to work in the fields on James Hopkinson's Plantation, Edisto Island, *Henry Moore, 1862* **(New-York Historical Society)**

When Federal forces occupied the Sea Islands off the coast of South Carolina in November 1861, almost all white inhabitants fled to the mainland, leaving behind a community of nearly 10,000 African-Americans. In "the Port Royal Experiment," the Federal government, Northern investors, missionaries, teachers, and the former slaves sought to determine the nature of the transition to freedom. Questions that arose over land ownership and control of labor during this "rehearsal for reconstruction" became central issues of the postwar era.

the postemancipation Southern economy. During the Civil War, in a series of experiments in Union-occupied areas scattered across the South, the first steps were taken toward addressing the interrelated problems of access to land and control of labor.

The most famous of these "rehearsals for Reconstruction" took place on the Sea Islands just off the coast of South Carolina. When the Union Navy occupied the area in November 1861, virtually all the white inhabitants fled to the mainland, leaving behind a community of some 10,000 slaves. When the planters departed, the slaves sacked the big houses and destroyed cotton gins; they then commenced planting corn and potatoes for their own use, but resisted growing the "slave crop," cotton. To them, freedom meant ownership of land, and the right to determine the use of their own labor.

Sea Island blacks, however, were not to chart their own course to "free labor," for in the navy's wake came a host of whites from the North: military officers, Treasury agents, Northern investors—eager to resume plantation agriculture at a time when the price of cotton had soared to unprecedented heights—and a group of young teachers and missionaries known as Gideon's Band. The entire Sea Island experiment took place in a blaze of publicity, as the area attracted newspapermen, government investigators, and others hoping to learn how the former slaves adjusted to freedom.

The most dramatic part of the story was the encounter between young reformers and the Sea Islands' freedpeople. The idealistic men and women from the North brought with them paternalistic attitudes toward blacks typical of the age, yet they genuinely desired to assist the former slaves to acquire education

Office of the Superintendent of Contrabands at Mitchelville,
Samuel A. Cooley, 1864. **(National Archives)**

Established by the Union Army as an "experiment in citizenship," Mitchelville differed from other military camps established for freedpeople living on the Sea Islands. It was developed as a town, with each home built on quarter-acre lots by its occupants, not by the military. By 1865, Mitchelville had about 1,500 inhabitants, an elected town supervisor and councilmen, laws regulating sanitation and community behavior, and provision for compulsory education.

Gideon's Band, c. 1862. **(Haverford College)**

In 1862, a group of black and white teachers and missionaries from the North, known as Gideon's Band, went to the South Carolina Sea Islands to work with the freedpeople. Named after the Old Testament warrior-prophet Gideon, they believed that a New England–style education would help former slaves become self-reliant, productive members of American society.

and take their place in the competitive world of the economic marketplace. Many sympathized with African-Americans' desire to acquire land.

Most government officials and Northern investors, however, believed the Sea Island experiment offered a golden opportunity to prove, as Northern plantation superintendent Edward S. Philbrick put it, that "the abandonment of slavery did not imply the abandonment of cotton," that blacks would work more efficiently and profitably as free laborers than as slaves. Rather than immediately acquiring land, they believed, the former slaves should work for wages and learn the discipline of the free market. "No man . . . appreciates property who does not work for it," Philbrick wrote. The freedpeople, however, believed that they had worked for the land during their 250 years of bondage. The Sea Island

Archeological materials excavated from Mitchelville, Hilton Head Island, South Carolina, c. 1862–1867. (Environmental and Historical Museum of Hilton Head)

Household items and personal belongings excavated from the freedpeople's village of Mitchelville offer a glimpse into the lifestyle of blacks who lived on the Sea Islands after gaining their freedom. Employed by the military as laborers on the island's cotton plantations, blacks entered into a cash economy and purchased goods at stores located on the island. Freedmen also acquired goods from the army and the American Missionary Association. In the 1980s, archeologists found a wide variety of materials at the Mitchelville site, including dishes, Union Army and civilian buttons, glass beads, pharmacy bottles, clay pipes, and spoon handles used to make indigenous sweet-water baskets. More expensive items like the ceramic transfer ware plate (fragment, upper left) and porcelain dolls (head, center) may have been appropriated by blacks from the island's abandoned plantation homes.

experiment produced many improvements in the lives of the area's black population, including access to schools and an improvement in their standard of living. However, it also brought disappointment, for when plantations abandoned by their owners were auctioned off by the federal government, only a few found their way into the hands of the former slaves.

Although contemporaries lavished attention upon it, the Sea Island experiment involved a far smaller area, and far fewer persons, than another rehearsal

Military auction of condemned property, Beaufort, South Carolina, 1865.
(Huntington Library, San Marino, California)

In June 1862, the federal government authorized the sale of abandoned lands at public auction. Men who had served in the U.S. military for at least three months could purchase such land by paying one-fourth of the purchase price at the time of the sale, with the balance due in three years. Although some former slaves pooled their resources to acquire land, Northern investors purchased most of the property. Note that several black soldiers attended the auction.

for Reconstruction, which took place in the Mississippi Valley. Here, as on the Sea Islands, slavery disintegrated when Northern soldiers occupied the area, and former slaves hoped to own the land. Unlike the situation in South Carolina, however, many slave owners remained on their plantations, declared their loyalty to the Union, and demanded that the army compel the slaves to remain at work.

Military officials, who established "contraband camps" for black refugees, had no desire to care permanently for large numbers of former slaves. They shared the belief that African-Americans should remain at work on the plantations. Thus, the military decreed that the former slaves must sign labor contracts with either planters who took an oath of loyalty or investors from the North. The former slaves would be paid wages and guaranteed access to schools, and corporal punishment was prohibited. But they could not leave the plantations without the permission of their employers, and the army would discipline those who refused to agree to plantation labor.

Reading the Contract to His Negroes, Grove Plantation, Port Royal, 1863. (Penn School Papers, Southern Historical Collection, University of North Carolina, Chapel Hill)

Freedpeople living on the Sea Islands and throughout the Union-occupied South labored for wages under terms of yearly contracts drawn up under army supervision. Although the contract labor system allowed production to resume by stabilizing labor relations during the war, it kept the vast majority of freedpeople poor and landless.

Inaugurated by Gen. Benjamin F. Butler in Louisiana, this system of "compulsory free labor" was extended to the entire Mississippi Valley, the home of more than half a million slaves, after the Union capture of Vicksburg in 1863. A halfway house between slavery and freedom, the system satisfied no one. Planters disliked not being able to use the whip to enforce discipline. They complained that the former slaves were unruly and refused to obey orders. The freedpeople, for their part, resented being forced to work for white employers, often their former owners, rather than being allowed access to land.

Whatever their differences, army officials and Southern planters seemed to agree that blacks should remain at work on the plantations. Only occasionally did glimmerings of a different policy appear. The largest laboratory in black economic independence was Davis Bend, a piece of land along the Mississippi River that contained the plantations of Confederate President Jefferson Davis and his brother Joseph. In 1863, Gen. Ulysses S. Grant decreed that Davis Bend should become a "Negro paradise," and directed that the entire area be set aside for the settlement of freedpeople, with the land assigned to groups who would work it without white supervision, and reap the profits. By 1865, Davis Bend had become a remarkable example of self-reliance, with successful cotton farming, a series of schools, and its own system of government, complete with elected judges and sheriffs.

Early in 1865, a new dimension to the troublesome questions of land and labor was added by Gen. William T. Sherman. After capturing Savannah at the conclusion of his famous March to the Sea, Sherman met with a group of the city's black leaders. The best guarantee of freedom, they told him, was "to have land, and turn it and till it by our own labor." Four days later, Sherman

Gen. William T. Sherman, c. 1863. (National Archives)

On January 16, 1865, Union general William T. Sherman, shortly after capturing Savannah at the end of his March to the Sea, issued Special Field Order 15, setting aside land on the Sea Islands and along the coasts of South Carolina and Georgia for black settlement. Intended to provide temporarily for the large number of former slaves following his army, Sherman's order nonetheless had the effect of raising blacks' expectations that the land would belong to them permanently.

issued Special Field Order 15, setting aside the Sea Islands and a portion of the South Carolina and Georgia coast extending thirty miles inland, for black settlement. Each family would receive forty acres of land, and Sherman later provided that the army could loan them mules. (Here, perhaps, lies the origin of the phrase "forty acres and a mule" that would soon echo throughout the South.) By June, some 40,000 freedpeople had been settled on 400,000 acres of "Sherman land."

In the spring of 1865, as the Civil War drew to a close, it was apparent that the federal government had not yet worked out its Reconstruction policy. No one knew whether the compulsory labor contracts of the Mississippi Valley or the grants of land to blacks at Davis Bend and by General Sherman, would set the pattern for shaping the transition from slave labor to free labor.

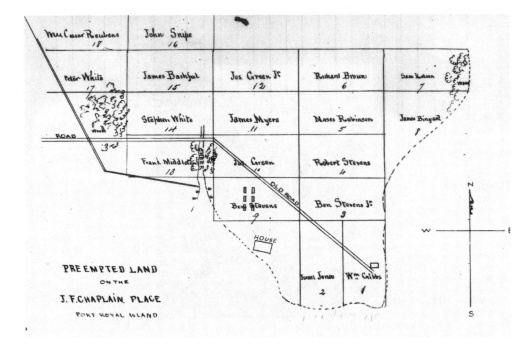

Diagram of plots selected for preemption by freedpeople on Port Royal Island,
South Carolina, January 25, 1864. (Cartography Division, National Archives)

Taking advantage of President Lincoln's order, issued in September 1863, to sell twenty-acre plots of land to black heads of family for not less than $1.25 an acre, eighteen freedpeople (seventeen men and one woman) selected plots on the John F. Chaplain plantation for purchase.

Lincoln Medal, designed by Franky Magniadas, gold, 1866.
(Manuscript Division, Library of Congress)

A medal commissioned in 1866 by a group of French republicans opposed to the regime of Napoleon III illustrates how Abraham Lincoln and the emancipated slave became international figures of liberty after the Civil War. The obverse features a profile portrait of Lincoln; the reverse has a monument dedicated to Lincoln, "the honest man who abolished slavery, restored the Union, and saved the Republic . . . ," flanked by a winged figure of victory, a black soldier, and a black youth holding the tools of education. Close by is another symbol of freedom—the ballot box.

Nor were the contours of political Reconstruction settled. Lincoln had established a new government in Louisiana under the 10 Percent Plan, but Congress had refused to seat its representatives. In his second inaugural address, in March, Lincoln called on the nation to bind up its wounds "with malice toward none and charity for all." He did not envision a Reconstruction based on harsh punishment of ex-Confederates. But leniency to whites, for Lincoln, did not mean abandoning concern for the rights of blacks. In his last speech, just a few days before his assassination, the president endorsed the idea of limited black suffrage for the Reconstruction South. He singled out former soldiers and those with some education as particularly deserving of the right to vote. This was the first time any American president had called for granting African-Americans the suffrage, and it illustrated the flexibility and capacity for growth that had always

SEA-ISLAND SCHOOL, No. 1.—ST. HELENA ISLAND. ESTABLISHED APRIL, 1862.

TEACHERS { MISS LAURA M. TOWNE, ELLEN MURRAY, MRS. HARRIET W. RUGGLES.   Supported by the Pennsylvania Branch.

EDUCATION AMONG THE FREEDMEN.

Pennsylvania Branch of the American Freedman's Union Commission.

PENNSYLVANIA FREEDMEN'S RELIEF ASSOCIATION,
No. 711 Sansom Street.

To the Friends of Education among the Freedmen.

As we enter upon our work for another year, we wish to present a statement of our plans and wants to the people.

The various organizations throughout the country having the education of the Freedmen in charge, have provided schools for 150,000 persons, in care of fourteen hundred teachers. The expense of supporting these schools has been borne by voluntary contributions.

It is frequently asked, Does not the Government accomplish this work through the "Freedmen's Bureau?" The simple answer is, No! The "Bureau" has no authority to employ teachers. The representatives of the "Bureau," from the honored Commissioner

Education Among the Freedmen, *pamphlet, Pennsylvania Freedmen's Relief Association, Philadelphia, c. 1864.* **(Library of Congress)**

The Pennsylvania Freedman's Relief Association circulated this pamphlet to solicit contributions for Sea Island School No. 1, later known as Penn School, on St. Helena Island, South Carolina. Laura Towne and Ellen Murray founded the school in 1862. The Association supplied them with a prefabricated structure to serve as a schoolhouse; Towne donated the bell. The school's academic program emulated the New England style by emphasizing traditional academics and the responsibilities of citizenship.

been the hallmarks of Lincoln's leadership. These were qualities, unfortunately, his successor lacked.

As the Civil War ended, the nation confronted a serious debate over Reconstruction. "Verily," as black abolitionist Frederick Douglass put it, "the work does not end with the abolition of slavery, but only begins."

Laura M. Towne

Laura M. Towne and pupils, 1866. (Penn School Papers, Southern Historical Collection, University of North Carolina, Chapel Hill)

Laura M. Towne (1825–1901), who devoted nearly forty years to educating the freedpeople, epitomized the spirit of New England reform after the Civil War. Born to a prosperous Pittsburgh family, Towne grew up in Boston and Philadelphia. As a young woman, she became an abolitionist.

In April 1862, under the auspices of the Port Royal Relief Committee of Philadelphia, Towne set out for the South Carolina Sea Islands, where nearly 10,000 slaves were now within Union lines. Like others involved in the Port Royal Experiment, she hoped to make the islands a showcase for freedom by demonstrating blacks' capacity for education and productive free labor. Towne shared the paternalistic attitudes toward blacks typical of the time, but she genuinely wanted to assist in the transition from slavery to freedom.

In September 1862, Towne and her friend Ellen Murray established Penn School on St. Helena Island. The school offered a traditional New England curriculum of arithmetic, reading and writing, geography, and classical languages. After 1870, it also trained black teachers. For several decades, Penn was the Sea Islands' only secondary school for blacks. Towne, who never married, volunteered her services and supported the school with contributions from Northern supporters.

While many Northerners returned home after the end of Reconstruction, Towne remained, operating the Penn School until her death. It continued to operate until the 1960s, and currently services as a community center.

Five Generations of an African-American Family, J. J. Smith's Plantation, South Carolina, *Timothy H. O'Sullivan, 1862.* (Library of Congress)

Even as an enslaved people, African-Americans maintained strong family ties. After emancipation, the family, together with the church, remained the foundation of the black community.

The Meaning of Freedom: Black and White Responses to the End of Slavery

Critical to the debate over Reconstruction were the complex reactions of Southerners, black and white alike, to the end of slavery. The central institution of antebellum Southern life, slavery was simultaneously a system of labor, a form of race relations, and the foundation of a distinctive regional ruling class. Its destruction led inevitably to conflict between blacks seeking to breathe substantive meaning into their freedom, and planters seeking to retain as much as possible of the old order. The South's nonslaveholding white majority found its way of life profoundly altered as well. Out of the conflict over the meaning of freedom arose new systems of labor and new kinds of relations between black and white Southerners.

"Freedom," said a black minister, "burned in the black heart long before freedom was born." But what did "freedom" mean? Rather than being a predetermined category or static concept, freedom itself became a terrain of conflict during Reconstruction, its definition open to different, often contradictory, interpretations, its content changing for whites as well as blacks in the aftermath of the Civil War.

To African-Americans, freedom meant independence from white control, autonomy both as individuals and as members of a community itself being transformed as a result of emancipation. Blacks relished the opportunity to flaunt their liberation from the innumerable regulations, significant and trivial, associated with slavery. They openly held mass meetings and religious services free of white oversight; they acquired dogs, guns, and liquor (all barred to them

Marriage certificate for Rufus Wright of the U.S. Colored Infantry and Elisabeth Turner, 1862. (National Archives)

Before the Civil War, slave marriages had no legal standing. During the war, blacks serving in the Union Army married under military authority. Henry M. Turner, one of the first black chaplains to serve in the Union Army, officiated at the wedding of Rufus Wright and Elisabeth Turner. On June 21, 1864, six months after his marriage, Wright died of abdominal wounds received in action at Petersburg. His widow's legal status enabled her to receive pension benefits from the federal government.

under slavery) and refused to yield the sidewalks to whites. No longer required to obtain a pass from their owner to travel, former slaves throughout the South left the plantations in search of better jobs, lost or distant family members, or simply a taste of personal freedom. Many moved to Southern towns and cities, where, it seemed, "freedom was free-er."

Before the war, free blacks had created a network of churches, schools, and mutual benefit societies, and slaves had forged a semiautonomous culture centered on the family and church. With freedom, these institutions were consolidated, expanded, and liberated from white supervision.

The family stood as the main pillar of the postemancipation black community. Under slavery, most blacks had lived in nuclear family units, although they faced the constant threat of separation from loved ones by sale. Reconstruction provided the opportunity to solidify their family ties. Freedpeople made remarkable efforts to locate loved ones from whom they had been separated under slavery. One Northern reporter in 1865 encountered a freedman who had walked more than 600 miles from Georgia to North Carolina, searching for his wife and children from whom he had been sold away. In addition, families who had been separated because their members belonged to different owners were now able to live together.

Control over their family life was essential to the former slaves' definition of freedom. Many freedwomen, preferring to devote more time to their families and wishing to be free from the supervision of white employers (which under slavery often led to sexual exploitation), refused to work any longer in the cotton fields. Black parents strenuously resisted efforts by many planters to force their children into involuntary labor through court-ordered apprenticeships, and insisted that they, rather than the employer, would decide when children went to school and when they labored in the fields.

At the same time, blacks withdrew almost entirely from white-controlled religious institutions (where they had been excluded from a role in church governance and often required to sit in the back pews during services). On the eve of the Civil War, 42,000 black Methodists worshipped in biracial South Carolina

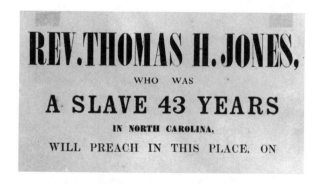

"Rev. Thomas H. Jones Will Preach,"
broadside, c. 1867. (Wadsworth Atheneum, Amistad Foundation)

After the war, African-Americans established their own churches and style of worship independent of the white community. Most southern blacks belonged to the African Methodist Episcopal and Baptist churches. Along with settled ministers, a number of itinerant preachers like the Rev. Thomas H. Jones also tended to the faithful.

HENRY M. TURNER

Rev. Henry M. Turner. (Schomburg Center
for Research in Black Culture)

Born to a poor free black family in New-berry, South Carolina, Henry M. Turner (1834–1915) learned to read and write while working as an office boy for a white lawyer. He later attended Trinity College in Balti-more. After preaching during the 1850s as a traveling Methodist evangelist, Turner was ordained a minister in the African Methodist Episcopal Church, and presided over Wash-ington, D.C.'s largest black congregation.

Turner served as a chaplain in a black regi-ment during the Civil War, and in 1865 went to Georgia, where he was briefly employed as a Freedmen's Bureau agent. He worked ener-getically to establish schools and churches for the former slaves. During Reconstruction, he was elected to the constitutional convention and the Georgia House of Representatives. Like other Republican leaders, Turner was threatened by the Ku Klux Klan, and his house was protected by armed guards.

After the end of Reconstruction, Turner became a bishop in the A.M.E. church, and served as president of Morris Brown College in Atlanta. Bitterly disappointed by the nation's abandonment of its commitment to racial equality, Turner became the era's most prominent advocate of black emigration from the United States. During the 1890s, he made four trips to Africa to promote set-tlement by black Americans. Turner died in Canada.

Interior View of the First African Baptist Church in Richmond, *engraving based on a sketch by William L. Sheppard,* Harper's Weekly, *June 27, 1874.*

Like other black churches throughout the South, the First African Baptist Church of Richmond played a central role in the black community. Founded in 1848, the church functioned as an autonomous black institution that served as a social and political gathering place, as well as a house of worship. Its pastor, the Rev. James Holmes, is seen preaching from an elevated pulpit to members of the congregation, which included nearly 4,000 people.

churches; by the end of Reconstruction only 600 remained. The rise of the independent black church, with Methodists and Baptists commanding the largest followings, redrew the religious map of the South.

The church played a central role in the black community; a place of worship, it also housed schools, social events, and political gatherings, and sponsored many of the fraternal and benevolent societies that sprang up during Reconstruction. Inevitably, black ministers came to play a major role in politics. More than 200 held public office during Reconstruction. "A man in this State," said Florida minister-legislator Charles H. Pearce, "cannot do his whole duty as a minister except as he looks out for the political interests of his people."

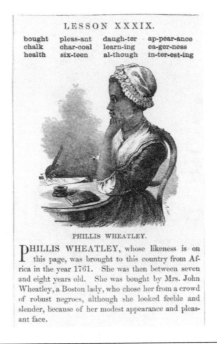

LESSON XXXIX.

bought	pleas-ant	daugh-ter	ap-pear-ance
chalk	char-coal	learn-ing	ea-ger-ness
health	six-teen	al-though	in-ter-est-ing

PHILLIS WHEATLEY.

PHILLIS WHEATLEY, whose likeness is on this page, was brought to this country from Africa in the year 1761. She was then between seven and eight years old. She was bought by Mrs. John Wheatley, a Boston lady, who chose her from a crowd of robust negroes, although she looked feeble and slender, because of her modest appearance and pleasant face.

Lesson page from The Freedman's Third Reader, *by Israel P. Warren, American Tract Society, Boston, 1866.* (Robert Morris)

Resembling texts used in Northern schools, books produced for the education of the freedpeople included lessons on spelling, reading, grammar, arithmetic, and history, as well as practical advice and moral instruction. Lesson thirty-nine of The Freedman's Third Reader *focused on Phillis Wheatley, an African-American poet who lived at the time of the American Revolution.*

Zion School for Colored Children, Charleston, South Carolina, *engraving based on sketch by Alfred R. Waud,* Harper's Weekly, *December 15, 1866.*

In June 1865, Francis L. Cardozo became head of the American Missionary Association's largest school in Charleston, which enrolled more than 1,000 pupils.

FRANCIS L. CARDOZO

Francis L. Cardozo, educator, minister, politician, engraving from William J. Simmons, Men of Mark: Eminent, Progressive, and Rising *(Cleveland, 1887), p. 433.*

The son of a prominent Jewish businessman of Charleston and his free black wife, Francis L. Cardozo (1837–1903) played a leading role in promoting black education in the city. After graduating in 1861 from the University of Glasgow in Scotland, he moved to Connecticut, where he served as a Congregationalist minister.

Cardozo returned to Charleston in 1865 as a teacher for the American Missionary Association, and soon was appointed to direct the association's educational activities in the city. In 1866, he was instrumental in the establishment of Avery Normal Institute and became its first superintendent. The school trained black teachers, "the object," Cardozo wrote, "for which I left all the superior advantages and privileges of the North and came South."

Although he claimed to have no desire to enter politics, Cardozo was elected to the constitutional convention of 1868, and he became the first black state official in South Carolina's history, holding the positions of secretary of state (1868–72) and treasurer (1872–76). He was defeated for reelection in 1876, when Democrats launched a campaign of violence that ended Republican rule in the state.

After the end of Reconstruction, Cardozo moved to Washington, where he served for twelve years as principal of a black high school. He died in Washington.

Interior of a freedman's school with an African-American teacher, c. 1870.
(Library of Congress)

During Reconstruction, the Freedmen's Bureau, missionary societies, and blacks themselves estab-
lished over 3,000 schools in the South, laying the foundation for public education in the region.
Many young men and women who attended freedman's schools became teachers who instructed the
next generation.

Another striking example of the freedpeople's quest for individual and community improvement was their thirst for education. Before the war, every
Southern state except Tennessee had prohibited the instruction of slaves. Now,
adults as well as children thronged the schools established during and after the
Civil War. Northern benevolent societies, the Freedmen's Bureau, and, after
1868, state governments, provided most of the funding for black education
during Reconstruction but the initiative often lay with African-Americans, who
pooled their meager resources and voluntarily taxed themselves to purchase
land, construct buildings, and hire teachers. Reconstruction also witnessed the
creation of the nation's first black colleges, including Fisk University in Ten-

Mother and Daughter Reading, Mt. Meigs, Alabama, *Rudolf Eickemeyer, 1890*.
(National Museum of American History, Smithsonian Institution)

Long after the war, freedpeople exhibited an almost unquenchable thirst for education, and learning took place outside of school as well as within. Illiteracy among blacks declined steadily as blacks continued to attend public schools and teach one another how to read and write.

Students at Hampton Institute, c.1870.
(Archival and Museum Collection, Hampton University)

In 1868, the American Missionary Association and the Freedmen's Bureau provided the funds to establish Hampton Normal and Agricultural Institute at Hampton, Virginia. Because Hampton's founder and first principal, Samuel C. Armstrong, believed economic advancement more important to the former slave than political involvement, the school emphasized "industrial training," such as sewing and printing, rather than liberal arts. Hampton also trained students to become industrial arts teachers; today, the university offers degrees in liberal arts, along with teacher and vocational training.

Howard University students on campus, 1870. (Moorland-Spingarn Research Center, Howard University Archives, Howard University)

Chartered by an act of Congress in 1867, Howard University offered black students preparatory and collegiate programs, including course work in law, medicine, education, and pharmacy. The university was named for Gen. Oliver O. Howard, head of the Freedmen's Bureau, who later served as the university's president. Today, the university remains a leading center of black education.

Fisk Jubilee Singers, c. 1875. (Fisk University, Special Collections)

Fisk University, one of the country's most important black institutions, was founded in 1866 as a liberal arts college in Nashville, Tennessee. Between 1871 and 1880, when the college faced financial difficulties, a group of students known as the Fisk Jubilee Singers staged a series of concerts that introduced traditional black spirituals to audiences in the northern United States, England, and Europe. Their successful tour raised enough money to help keep the college open.

The Colored National Convention held at Nashville, April 5, 6, and 7,
engraving from Frank Leslie's Illustrated Newspaper, *May 6, 1876.*

During Reconstruction, Southern blacks organized numerous state and national conventions that demanded equal rights, education, and economic opportunities. Many of Reconstruction's prominent black leaders emerged from these conventions.

nessee, Hampton Institute in Virginia, and Howard University in the nation's capital. Initially, these institutions emphasized the training of black teachers, and by 1869, blacks outnumbered whites among the approximately 3,000 men and women teaching the freedpeople in the South.

The desire for autonomy also shaped African-Americans' economic definition of freedom. Blacks wished to take control of the conditions under which they labored, and carve out the greatest degree of economic independence. Most refused to work any longer in gangs under the direction of an overseer, and generally preferred renting land to working for wages. Above all, economic freedom meant owning land of their own.

In the aftermath of the Civil War, many former slaves insisted that through their unpaid labor, they had acquired a right to a portion of their owners' land.

"The property which they hold," declared an Alabama black convention, "was nearly all earned by the sweat of *our* brows." In 1865, in some parts of the South, blacks seized abandoned land or refused to leave plantations, insisting that the property belonged to them. On the property of a Tennessee planter, former slaves not only claimed to be "joint heirs" to the estate but, the owner complained, took up residence "in the rooms of my house." Others, citing the Freedmen's Bureau Act and the land distribution policy announced by General Sherman, expected the federal government to guarantee them access to land. This quest for economic independence put the former slaves at odds with former owners seeking to restore plantation discipline and with many Northerners committed to reinvigorating Southern cotton production as quickly as possible.

If the goal of autonomy inspired African-Americans to withdraw from institutions controlled by whites and attempt to work out their economic destinies by themselves, in public life "freedom" meant inclusion rather than separation. Recognition of their equal rights as citizens quickly emerged as the animating impulse of black politics. Throughout 1865, blacks organized mass meetings, parades, petitions, and conventions demanding equality before the law and the

Secret Meeting of Southern Unionists, *engraving based on a sketch by Alfred R. Waud,* Harper's Weekly, *August 4, 1866.*

According to the accompanying article, this sketch depicted a meeting in Louisiana of Union men who resented Andrew Johnson's Reconstruction policies that "returned the power to the hands of the old dominant slave-owning class."

The Ruins of Richmond, *photograph, Alexander Gardner, 1865.*
(Chicago Historical Society)

At the close of the Civil War, the main business section of Richmond, the Confederate capital, lay in ruins, resulting from devastating fires set by looters, merchants, and Confederate troops fleeing the advance of the Union Army.

right to vote. The end of slavery, they insisted, enabled America for the first time to live up to the full implications of its democratic creed by abandoning racial proscription and absorbing blacks fully into the civil and political order.

If former slaves saw Reconstruction as heralding a new era of autonomy and equality, most Southern whites reacted to military defeat and emancipation with dismay. To be sure, a minority of whites welcomed the North's victory. These were wartime Unionists, despised as traitors by supporters of the Confederacy. In parts of the Southern hill country, far from the plantation belt, some nonslave-holding farmers had opposed secession from the beginning, while many others grew disaffected as the war progressed, casualties mounted, and economic dislocation increased. Confederate policies like the exemption from military service of one white man for every twenty slaves on a plantation, convinced many yeomen that the Civil War had become "a rich man's war and a poor man's fight." These Unionists saw Reconstruction as an opportunity to oust from power the planter elite that had led the South into the disaster of secession and war.

Most white Southerners, however, had supported the Confederacy and emerged from the Civil War in a state of shock. "The demoralization is complete," wrote a Georgia girl. "We are whipped, there is no doubt about it." The

Decorating the Graves of Rebel Soldiers, *engraving based on a drawing by William L. Sheppard,* Harper's Weekly, August 17, 1867.

After the Civil War, Southerners and Northerners alike engaged in private and public mourning cere-monies for the war dead. On May 31, 1867, citizens of Richmond, acting under the auspices of the Hollywood Memorial Association, visited Hollywood Memorial Cemetery overlooking the James River to decorate thousands of Confederate graves with flowers. The association, founded by a group of Rich-mond women, had raised enough funds to transfer over 16,000 Confederate dead from Northern ceme-teries for reburial in Richmond. The annual tradition of honoring the dead evolved into Memorial Day.

appalling loss of life, a disaster without parallel in the American experience, affected all classes of Southerners. Nearly 260,000 men died for the Confed-eracy—over one-fifth of the South's adult white male population. Many more were wounded, some maimed for life. (In addition, 37,000 blacks perished in the Union army, as did tens of thousands more in camps for refugees and on Confederate army labor gangs.) The widespread destruction of work animals, farm buildings, and machinery ensured that economic revival would be slow and painful. Between 1860 and 1870, while farm output expanded in the rest of the nation, the South experienced precipitous declines in the value of farm land, the number of farm animals, and the amount of acreage under cultivation. Confed-erate Gen. Braxton Bragg returned to his "once prosperous" Alabama home to

Upland family near Cedar Mountain, Virginia, c. 1865. (Library of Congress)

Upland Southern farmers, most of whom owned few or no slaves before the Civil War, experienced great changes during Reconstruction as they shifted from subsistence to commercial farming. Despite new links to a market economy, many remained geographically isolated and culturally distinct from lowland Southerners.

find "*all, all* was lost, except my debts." Bragg and his wife, a woman "raised in affluence," lived for a time in a slave cabin.

During the Civil War, the South's white yeomen suffered devastating losses, which threatened the economic independence to which they had previously been accustomed. Small farmers had filled the ranks of the Confederate army and suffered the bulk of casualties, leaving many farms to be tilled by widows. Lying at the war's strategic crossroads, portions of upcountry Tennessee, Alabama, Georgia, and Mississippi had been laid waste by the march of opposing armies. Wartime devastation set in motion a train of events that per-

Farmers with cotton in the courthouse square, Marietta, Georgia, 1880.
(Georgia Department of Archives and History)

Before the Civil War, most white Southerners engaged in subsistence farming, producing enough food to support their own families. After the war, they turned to cotton production as a means of livelihood, permanently altering their self-sufficient way of life. Civil War debts, crop failures, rising taxes, and falling farm prices led increasing numbers of them to lose their land and become tenant farmers.

manently altered the yeomanry's self-sufficient way of life. Before the Civil War, most yeomen had concentrated on raising food for their families and grew little cotton. Plunged into debt by the war, with fences, farm animals, and buildings often destroyed, many small farmers saw their plight exacerbated by successive crop failures in early Reconstruction. Needing to borrow money for the seed, implements, and livestock required to resume farming, many fell into debt and were forced to take up the growing of cotton. As the price of cotton fell, their growing dependence on the market economy produced an ever-increasing spiral of debt. White farmers, who cultivated only one-tenth of the South's cotton

The Lost Cause, *W. E. Omsley of New Orleans, 1868.*
(Louisiana Collection, Howard-Tilton Library, Tulane University)

After the Civil War, many Southern whites reacted to the harsh realities of defeat by developing a romanticized view of the past that became known as the "Lost Cause." Popular prints often depicted the Confederacy's defeat as a great tragedy; a lengthy text accompanying the image identified the "Church and the Negro" as those responsible for causing "the late great war."

crop in 1860, by the mid-1870s were growing 40 percent, and many who had owned their land had fallen into dependency as tenants.

Planter families also faced profound changes in the aftermath of the war. Many women had taken on new roles during the Civil War, assuming greater and greater authority for managing slaves and plantations while their husbands were absent or serving as nurses, teachers, accountants, and in other professions previously limited to men. The death of so many soldiers meant that women would continue to fill these unaccustomed roles. Many relished and hoped to preserve their new independence, even as they sought to help their husbands and sons adapt to the reality of military defeat, and continued to adhere to the nineteenth-century South's strict division of the proper spheres of white men and women.

Planter families were devastated by the loss of their slaves and life savings, to the extent that they had patriotically invested in Confederate bonds. Some, whose slaves departed the plantation, for the first time found themselves com-

The Burial of Latanè, *engraving by A. G. Campbell after a painting*
by William D. Washington, 1864, published by William Pate, New York, 1868.
(**Virginia Historical Society**)

Perhaps the most popular image of the Lost Cause, The Burial of Latanè, *appealed to Southerners seeking security in memories of an idealized past as they faced the disruptions and uncertainties of the post–Civil War era. The harmonious scene depicts a group of valiant Southern women and loyal slaves burying William D. Latanè, a young Confederate captain, in a plantation cemetery far from home. Latanè died as the only casualty of J. E. B. Stuart's famous ride around Union forces in 1862. During the war, the original painting was exhibited in the Virginia State Capitol, where a bucket was reportedly placed in front of it to collect donations for the war effort.*

Memorial hair wreath made by Jean-netta E. Conrad, Harrisonburg, Virginia, c. 1870. (Museum of the Confederacy)

A single branched spray of hair flowers contains locks of hair from prominent Confederates such as Jefferson Davis, J. E. B. Stuart, and Robert E. Lee. The Victorian custom of collecting hair from loved ones or famous people and fashioning it into jewelry or decorative ornaments was widely practiced throughout America during the second half of the nineteenth century.

Carving, maker unknown, stone, c. 1875. (Tennessee State Museum Collection)

A carving that juxtaposes Confederate general Robert E. Lee with the crucified Christ illustrates the extent to which the Lost Cause had acquired religious overtones by the 1870s. By then, white Southerners had developed a pantheon of godlike heroes with an elaborate body of legend to help sustain the memory of the Confederacy.

pelled to do physical labor. Facing what one planter called "a joyless future of probable ignominy, poverty, and want," as many as 10,000 slave owners abandoned their homes after the war, hoping to emigrate to the North or Europe or to reestablish themselves as planters in Brazil, where slavery still existed. Others sought to "drown our troubles in a sea of gaiety," reviving aristocratic social life as if nothing had changed, or retreating into nostalgia for the Old South and a romanticized notion of the Confederate experience that celebrated the struggle for Southern independence as a noble Lost Cause. In 1865 and 1866 many Southerners threw themselves into memorial associations that established Confederate cemeteries and monuments throughout the region. Organizations like the Southern Historical Association and magazines like *The Land We Love* worked strenuously to keep alive the memory of the struggle for Southern independence. The Lost Cause did not reach its heyday until the 1880s and 1890s, but during Reconstruction many Southerners brooded over Confederate defeat and railed against the ways of the North.

The Great Labor Question From a Southern Point of View, *cartoon,*
Winslow Homer, **Harper's Weekly,** *July 29, 1865.*
(Schomburg Center for Research in Black Culture)

A cartoon criticizing the postwar attitudes of many Southern whites toward freedpeople depicts a leisured white planter admonishing his former slave, "My boy, we've toiled and taken care of you long enough—now, you've got to work!"

In a sense, the most arduous task facing former slave owners was adjusting to the world of free labor. For those accustomed to the power of command, the normal give-and-take of employer and employee was difficult to accept. Behavior entirely normal in the North, such as a freedman leaving the employ of a Georgia farmer because "he thought he could do better," provoked cries of outrage and charges of ingratitude.

Among white Southerners, the question "Will the free Negro work?" became an all-absorbing obsession in 1865 and 1866. It was widely believed that African-Americans, naturally lazy, would work only when coerced. Charges of "indolence" were often directed not against blacks unwilling to work at all, but at those who preferred to labor for themselves rather than signing contracts with whites. In the strange logic of a plantation society, African-Americans who sought to become self-sufficient farmers seemed not examples of industrious-ness, but demoralized freedmen unwilling to work—work, that is, under white supervision on a plantation.

Labor contract, January 10, 1866. (Caroliniana Library, University of South Carolina)

The labor system that replaced slavery involved yearly contracts drawn up between freedpeople and planters. In addition to minimum pay, contracts usually stipulated that laborers remain on the plan-tation throughout the term of employment; some employers supplied laborers with food, medicine, and clothing. As noted on the contract, illiterate laborers signed the agreement by placing an "X" next to their names.

Gen. Oliver Otis Howard, c. 1865. (National Archives)

Union Army general Oliver O. Howard, who opposed slavery before the Civil War, directed the Freedmen's Bureau from 1865 to 1874. He believed that a combination of education, citizenship rights, and self-help would enable the freedpeople to take their place in American society. In 1869, Howard helped found the university in Washington, D.C., that bears his name.

Planters understood that the questions of land and labor were intimately interrelated. Many were convinced, a Northern visitor reported, "that so long as they retain possession of their lands they can oblige the negroes to work on such terms as they please." They rejected the former slaves' equation of freedom and economic autonomy. "Our negroes have a fall, a tall fall ahead of them," wrote Mississippi planter Samuel Agnew. "They will learn that freedom and independence are different things. A man may be free and yet not independent."

Between the planters' need for a disciplined labor force and the freed-people's quest for autonomy, conflict was inevitable. Planters sought through written labor contracts to reestablish their autonomy over every aspect of their laborers' lives. But former slaves rejected the idea of white supervision. Conflict was endemic on plantations throughout the South. Blacks, planters complained, insisted on setting their own hours of labor, worked at their own pace, and demanded the right to conduct their personal lives as they saw fit. Meanwhile, the withdrawal of many black women from field labor and the refusal of men to

Office of the Freedmen's Bureau, Memphis, Tennessee,
engraving, **Harper's Weekly,** *June 2, 1866.*

In 1865, Congress established the Freedmen's Bureau to provide assistance to former slaves during the post–Civil War period. Among other responsibilities, bureau agents settled disputes between black and white Southerners. The Bureau's jurisdiction in civil matters eventually became a point of controversy.

work as long hours as they had been forced to do under slavery, produced a pervasive "labor shortage" in the South. To attract workers, many planters were forced to raise wages and offer land free of charge for garden plots.

With planters seeking to establish a labor system as close to slavery as possible, and former slaves demanding economic autonomy and access to land, it fell to the Freedmen's Bureau to attempt to mediate between the contending parties. The Bureau's myriad responsibilities included establishing schools for freedmen, providing aid to the destitute, aged, ill, and insane, adjudicating disputes among blacks and between the races, and attempting to secure for blacks and white Unionists equal justice from postwar Southern courts. Much of the

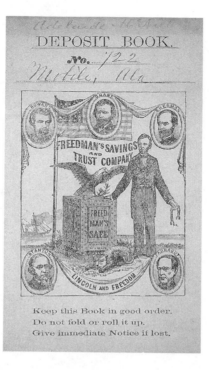

Savings book from the Freedman's Saving and Trust Company, c. 1870.
(National Archives)

In 1865, Congress established the Freedman's Saving and Trust Company as a private corporation to encourage thrift among the former slaves. Black individuals, families, church groups, fraternal orders, and civic organizations deposited nearly two million dollars in branch banks located throughout the South. The bank failed in 1874 and thousands of depositors lost their savings.

Bureau's activity, however, centered on overseeing the transition from slave to free labor.

Some Bureau officials believed that the former slaves must sign labor contracts and go back to work on the plantations. Others, like Gen. Rufus Saxton, who directed the agency's activities in South Carolina in 1865, sympathized strongly with blacks' aspiration to own land. In the summer of 1865, however, President Andrew Johnson, who had succeeded Lincoln, ordered land in federal hands returned to its former owners. A series of confrontations followed, notably in South Carolina and Georgia, where blacks were forcibly evicted from the land they had been settled on by General Sherman. In the end, the vast

Cotton pickers, 1867. (New-York Historical Society)

During the Reconstruction era, sharecropping emerged as the dominant system of labor in the South. In sharecropping, individual families signed contracts with landowners to work a specific piece of land; the system placed a premium on labor, forcing many women and children to work in the fields. Share-croppers kept one-third to one-half of the crop for themselves and the remainder went to the landowner. Although the system afforded workers some degree of autonomy, it kept most in a state of poverty and impeded the South's economic development.

majority of rural freedpeople remained propertyless and poor, with no alternative but to work as laborers on white-owned plantations. "This is not the condition of really free men," declared a protest meeting on the Sea Islands. The Freedmen's Bureau attempted to ensure that labor contracts were equitable, and that the former slaves were free to leave their jobs once the contract had expired. But the ideal of forty acres and a mule was dead. The result was a deep sense of

Union Army recruitment poster, Come and Join Us Brothers,
lithograph, by P.S. Duval & Son, Philadelphia, 1863. (Chicago Historical Society)

When the Union Army began to recruit black men into its ranks, it used imagery that conveyed the
dignity of military service. As illustrated by this poster, black soldiers served in segregated units under
white officers, reassuring Northerners who feared the arming of black Americans. By war's end, more
than 180,000 blacks had served in the army and nearly 40,000 had lost their lives.

Union banner, made by Rachel Simon Lewis of Richmond, silk and wool threads with paint on linen, 1855. **(Chicago Historical Society)**

During the Civil War, some white Southerners remained loyal to the Union. The Lewis family of Richmond hid this banner behind a mirror during the war, and when Federal troops entered the city on April 3, 1865, they hung it in front of their home as a sign of victory. The banner commemorates George Washington's victory at the battle of Yorktown, the last major battle of the American Revolutionary War.

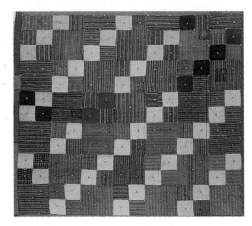

Pieced quilt attributed to an African-American maker, linsey-woolsey, mid-nineteenth century. (Valentine Museum, Richmond, Virginia)

Despite the hardships of slavery, African-Americans maintained a rich tradition of art and handicrafts. When making quilts, they followed patterns reflecting a variety of African, European, and American influences. This quilt, passed down through several generations of a black family, features a four-patch checkerboard design dating from the Colonial era.

Crazy quilt (detail), *maker unknown, silk and velvet, c. 1870.* **(Valentine Museum, Richmond, Virginia)**

A quilt from the postwar era with an image of Robert E. Lee in the center illustrates how white Southerners incorporated images of the Lost Cause into their daily lives. The quilt also contains miniature Confederate flags and memorial ribbons.

A Visit from the Old Mistress, *by Winslow Homer, oil on canvas, 1876.* (National Museum of American Art, Smithsonian Institution, Gift of William T. Evans)

American artist Winslow Homer captured the tensions and ambiguities of Reconstruction's new social order when he depicted an imaginary meeting between a Southern white woman and her former slaves. Homer, an artist-correspondent during the Civil War, placed his subjects on an equal footing yet maintained a space of separation between the races. He exhibited the painting to acclaim at the Paris Universal Exposition in 1878, yet white critics in Virginia taunted him for depicting blacks, and some African-Americans criticized him for portraying exclusively poor, rural blacks rather than members of the growing black professional class living in urban areas.

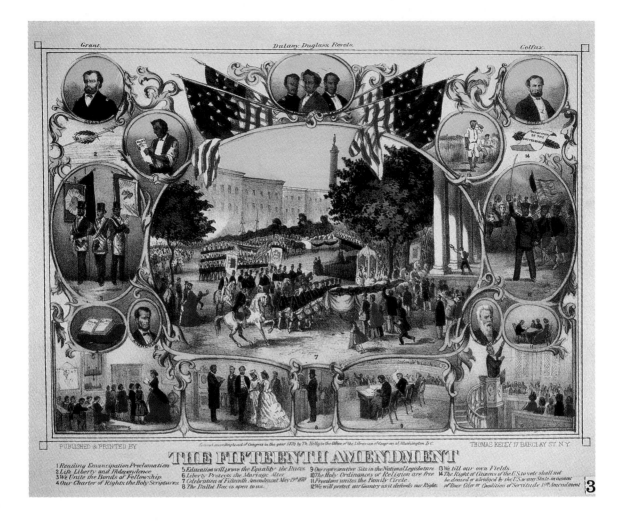

The Fifteenth Amendment,
color lithograph by Thomas Kelly, New York, 1870. (Chicago Historical Society)

As depicted in this lithograph, the ratification of the Fifteenth Amendment to the U.S. Constitution inspired celebrations by African-Americans and their antislavery allies. The amendment prohibited states from abridging the right to vote because of race, although it allowed other restrictions, such as those based on education, property, and sex to remain in effect. Republicans applauded the measure as the culmination of the struggle for black rights while Democrats described it as the "crowning" act of a Radical conspiracy to promote racial equality.

"*The Shackle Broken by the Genius of Freedom,*"
color lithograph by E. Sachs & Company, Baltimore, 1874. (Wadsworth Atheneum)

A print celebrating the history of black freedom depicts the famous address by South Carolina Representative Robert B. Elliott in favor of the bill that became the Civil Rights Act of 1875. The print also includes a portrait of the bill's author, Charles Sumner, an image of Lincoln, and an optimistic view of the future with a scene of black family life captioned "American Slave Labour Is of the Past— Free Labour Is of the Present—We Toil for Our Children and Not for Those of Others."

Carpetbag, tapestry wool, mid-nineteenth century.
(Valentine Museum, Richmond, Virginia)

Widely used as travel bags in the mid-nineteenth century, carpetbags became associated with Northern white Republicans who moved South after the Civil War. "Carpetbagger," a derisive term devised by Reconstruction's opponents, has remained part of the vocabulary of American politics.

"Sambo" clock, maker unknown, painted cast iron, c. 1875. (Chicago Historical Society)

As white Americans grew weary of Reconstruction, derogatory images of African-Americans became more prevalent and accepted in the North as well as in the South. A mantle clock made in Connecticut portrays a black man as "Sambo," a naive, clownish figure that remained a familiar American stereotype well into the twentieth century.

Republican and Democratic election tickets, 1868–71. (Mississippi Archives)

Election tickets from Mississippi list a number of candidates, illustrating the fact that the nineteenth-century electorate generally voted along straight party lines. Citizens voted by dropping election tickets into a ballot box.

Ku Klux Klan flag, painted taffeta, c. 1866.
(Chicago Historical Society)

As part of the attack against blacks and white Republicans, the Klan used a variety of menacing symbols to frighten its potential victims. A flag from Tennessee bears a Satanic dragon and a Latin motto referring to African-Americans: "Because it always is, Because it is everywhere, because it is abominable."

Ku Klux Klan robe and hood, appliqué and painted linen, Lincoln County, Tennessee, c. 1866. (Chicago Historical Society)

As they carried out their campaign of terror, Klan members disguised themselves in hooded robes. Although the Klan did not have an official uniform at this time, the robes often featured astrological symbols like stars and moons. The appliqué face of this hood includes eye holes trimmed with blue fabric. The Klan's more familiar white robes came into being in the 1920s, when the organization experienced a revival.

A COTTON PLANTATION ON THE MISSISSIPPI.

A Cotton Plantation on the Mississippi,
color lithograph by Currier & Ives, 1884. (Library of Congress)

A popular print based on an original painting by William Walker, a Southern genre artist, illustrates how a more positive view of the South emerged as the issues of the Civil War and Reconstruction began to recede into memory. Walker's scene illustrates the ideology of the "New South" by depicting a prosperous plantation manned by industrious blacks working under the supervision of benevolent whites.

Cotton Gin in Use, *woodcut from* DeBow's Review, *October 1867.* (Library of Congress)

Despite the changes wrought by emancipation, cotton production in the South remained much the same as before. As depicted in an illustration from DeBow's Review, *black laborers working with animal-powered cotton gins cleaned the harvested cotton, then baled it for shipment to market. The article in which the illustration appeared, "In Lieu of Labor," urged postwar Southern farmers to rely more on machinery and less on contract laborers.*

Interior View of Ginning Mills at Knox Plantation near Charleston, South Carolina,
George Barnard, 1874. (Charleston Museum, Charleston, South Carolina)

Sharecroppers brought harvested cotton to a central gin house where it could be cleaned for market. Most cotton produced in the South during the Reconstruction era was shipped to in the textile mills of New England and Britain.

The Sugar Harvest in Louisiana, *engraving based on a sketch*
by Alfred R. Waud, **Harper's Weekly,** *October 30, 1875.*

In the Deep South, sugar workers continued to labor in closely supervised gangs after the Civil War.
The system persisted because each plantation had its own steam-powered sugar mill that required a large
crop and labor force to insure economic viability. An influx of Northern capital allowed sugar planters to
pay their workers in cash, but conflicts between owners and workers arose over wages and discipline.

betrayal, which survived among the freedpeople and their descendants long after
the end of Reconstruction.

Out of the conflict on the plantations, and with black landownership all but
precluded, new systems of labor emerged in the different regions of the South.
Sharecropping came to dominate the cotton South and much of the tobacco belt
of Virginia and North Carolina. A compromise between blacks' desire for land and
planters' for labor discipline, sharecropping allowed each black family to work its
own tenant farm, with the crop divided with the owner at the end of the year. It
guaranteed the planters a stable resident labor force, and the former slaves the
right to work without outside supervision. In the Louisiana sugar region, an influx

Rice fanner, sweet grass, mid-nineteenth century.
(Charleston Museum, Charleston, South Carolina)

Rice mortar and pestle, heart of pine, nineteenth century.
(South Carolina State Museum)

African-Americans who worked in the South's rice industry used traditional methods and tools developed in West Africa and brought with them in the diaspora. They used large, shallow baskets, known as fanners, to winnow or separate the grain from the chaff, and a mortar and pestle to husk the grain.

Rice Culture on the Ogeechee, Near Savannah, Georgia, *engraving based on a sketch by Alfred R. Waud,* Harper's Weekly, January 5, 1867.

During Reconstruction, a variety of labor systems coexisted on rice plantations but nearly all included the traditional task system developed in antebellum days. In the task system, laborers, rather than working in gangs under an overseer, performed assigned tasks after which they hunted, fished, or grew crops on their own time. As a result, rice workers enjoyed a greater degree of autonomy than most former slaves, who worked under tighter controls.

of Northern capital allowed for the repair of equipment and the resumption of production. Gang labor survived the end of slavery, with blacks working for wages higher than those offered elsewhere in the South, and allowed access to garden plots to grow their own food. By contrast, in the rice kingdom of coastal South Carolina and Georgia, planters were unable to acquire the large amounts of capital necessary to repair the irrigation systems and threshing machinery that were destroyed by the war, and blacks continued to demand access to the land they had occupied in 1865. In the end, the great plantations fell to pieces, and blacks were able to acquire small pieces of land and take up self-sufficient farming.

Richland Cotton Plantation store, Mississippi, c. 1868. (Wadsworth Atheneum)

After the Civil War, country stores offered a variety of goods shipped from the North. Farmers and sharecroppers often could not afford to make a purchase except "on credit" at exorbitant interest rates. Widespread use of credit increased debt and poverty among rural Southerners during the Reconstruction era.

A nursemaid and her charge, from a daguerreotype, c. 1865.
(Valentine Museum, Richmond, Virginia)

African-Americans found a wider variety of employment opportunities in cities than in rural areas but the vast majority worked as manual laborers. Many black women worked as domestic servants.

Like white small farmers, blacks' economic opportunities after the Civil War were limited by the region's credit system and by a world market in which the price of farm products suffered a prolonged decline. To obtain supplies from merchants, both black and white farmers were forced to pledge a portion of the cotton crop as collateral—a system known as the crop lien. Since interest rates were extremely high, and the price of cotton was falling, many farmers found themselves still mired in debt after their portion of the crop was marketed at year's end.

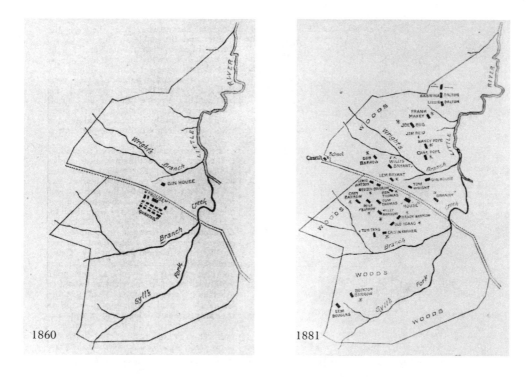

Maps of the Barrow Plantation, Scribner's Monthly, *April 1881.*

Two maps illustrate the effects of emancipation on plantation life in the South. In 1860, slaves lived in communal quarters near the owner's house, subject to frequent contact and strict control. Twenty years later, former slaves working as sharecroppers lived away from "The House" on separate plots of land and had their own church and school. However, the "Gin house," where cotton was cleaned, remained in the same location, central to the economic life of the plantation.

Even as the rural South, locked into a one-crop mold, stagnated economically, Southern cities experienced remarkable growth after the Civil War. As railroads penetrated the interior, they spurred the growth of market centers like Atlanta, and smaller towns like Selma and Macon, enabling merchants there to trade directly with the North and bypass coastal cities that had traditionally monopolized Southern commerce. A new urban middle class of merchants, railroad promoters, and bankers reaped the benefits of the spread of cotton production in the postwar South.

African-Americans at Montevideo Plantation, c. 1898.
(Howard-Tilton Memorial Library, Tulane University)

In 1898, Mary Jones's eldest son, Charles C. Jones, Jr., published Montevideo-Maybank, or, the Family Life of the Rev. Charles Colcock Jones, D.D. *The book, illustrated with photographs of his family's plantation in Georgia, paid tribute to a way of life destroyed by the Civil War. Blacks living at Montevideo thirty-five years after emancipation descended from slaves once owned by the Jones family.*

Thus, Reconstruction witnessed profound changes in the lives of Southerners black and white, rich and poor. In place of the antebellum world of master and slave, the postwar South was peopled by new social classes—landowning employers, black and white sharecroppers, cotton-producing yeomen, urban entrepreneurs. Each of these groups would turn to Reconstruction politics in an attempt to shape to its own advantage the meaning of freedom and the consequences of emancipation.

MARY J. JONES

Mary J. Jones, c. 1865. (Howard-Tilton Memorial Library, Tulane University)

Like other members of the planter class, Mary J. Jones (1808–69) found her life transformed during and after the Civil War. Although the Jones family prided themselves on their paternalistic regard for more than one hundred slaves, emancipation irrevocably altered relations between whites and blacks on the Jones plantations.

Born to a planter family in Liberty County, Georgia, Jones was educated at local women's academies. In 1830, she married her first cousin, Dr. Charles Colcock Jones, a Presbyterian clergyman who devoted much of his life to the religious education of African-Americans.

After her husband's death in 1863, Mary Jones, like other Southern white women of the era, found herself with new responsibilities. With her two sons serving in the Con-

federate army and then living far from home, she struggled on her own to operate the family's three plantations.

In a series of letters written to her children (and published in 1972 in the acclaimed volume *The Children of Pride*), Jones described the difficulties of operating a plantation in early Reconstruction—crop failures, black resistance to white supervision, constant disputes over labor contracts. She had considered her former slaves "friends," she wrote, but now they were "only laborers under contract, [with] only the law between us."

In 1867, at her children's urging but with great reluctance, Mary Jones rented her plantation to former slaves and moved to New Orleans to live with her married daughter. She died there two years later.

Reconstruction, *lithograph published by Horatio Bateman of New York, 1867.* (Library of Congress)

An elaborate allegory with religious overtones embodies the lofty ideals associated with the early years of Reconstruction. The United States, depicted as a colossal pavillion, is literally being reconstructed as the old columns of slavery are replaced with Justice, Liberty, and Education. The heavens are filled with portraits of American heroes from the North and South, including John C. Calhoun, Daniel Webster, and Abraham Lincoln. Below is a vignette with black and white infants sleeping beneath an American eagle holding a streamer that reads "All men are born free and equal."

The Politics of Reconstruction and the Origins of Civil Rights

Robert E. Lee surrendered the Army of Northern Virginia on April 9, 1865, effectively ending the Civil War. Five days later, President Lincoln was mortally wounded by an assassin. To his successor, Vice President Andrew Johnson, fell the task of overseeing the restoration of the Union. The only senator from a seceding state to remain at his post in 1861, Johnson had been appointed military governor of Tennessee by President Lincoln and was placed on the Republican ticket in 1864 as a symbol of Republican plans to extend their organization into the South. But Johnson proved incapable of providing the nation with enlightened leadership or meeting the North's demand for a just and lasting Reconstruction.

In personality and outlook, Johnson was ill suited for the responsibilities he now shouldered. A lonely, stubborn man, he was intolerant of criticism and unable to compromise. He lacked Lincoln's political skills and keen sense of Northern public opinion. Moreover, while Johnson had supported emancipation during the war, he held deeply racist views. A self-proclaimed spokesman for the poor white farmers of the South, he condemned the old planter aristocracy, but believed African-Americans had no role to play in Reconstruction.

With Congress out of session until December, Johnson in May 1865 outlined his plan for reuniting the nation. He issued a series of proclamations that inaugurated the period of Presidential Reconstruction (1865–67). Johnson offered a pardon to all Southern whites, except Confederate leaders and wealthy planters (and most of these subsequently received individual pardons), who took

Selling a Freeman to Pay His Fine at Monticello, Florida, *engraving based on a drawing by James E. Taylor,* Frank Leslie's Illustrated Newspaper, *January 19, 1867.*

The Black Codes, a series of laws passed by Southern states to define freedmen's rights and responsibilities, imposed serious restrictions upon former slaves. For example, Florida's code made disobedience a crime, and blacks who broke labor contracts could be whipped, pilloried, and sold for up to one year's labor. The Black Codes created an uproar among many Northerners, who considered them to be another form of slavery.

an oath of allegiance. He also appointed provisional governors and ordered state conventions held, elected by whites alone. Apart from the requirement that they abolish slavery, repudiate secession, and abrogate the Confederate debt—all inescapable consequences of Southern defeat—the new governments were granted a free hand in managing their affairs. Previously, Johnson had spoken of severely punishing "traitors," and most white Southerners believed his proposals surprisingly lenient.

Radical Republicans criticized Johnson's plan of Reconstruction for ignoring the rights of the former slaves. But at the outset, most Northerners believed the policy deserved a chance to succeed. The conduct of the new Southern governments elected under Johnson's program, however, turned most of the Republican North against the president.

Johnson assumed that when elections were held for governors, legislators, and congressmen, Unionist yeomen would replace the planters who had led the South into secession. In fact, white voters by and large returned members of the old elite to power. Alarmed by the apparent ascendancy of "rebels," Republicans were further outraged by reports of violence directed against former slaves and Northern visitors in the South. But what aroused the most opposition were laws passed by the new Southern governments, attempting to regulate the lives of the former slaves. Known as the Black Codes, these laws did grant the freedpeople certain rights, such as the right to own property and bring suit in court. African-Americans could not, however, testify against whites, serve on juries or in state militias, or vote.

Responding to planters' demands that the freedpeople be forced back to work on the plantations, the Black Codes required blacks to sign yearly labor contracts. The unemployed were declared vagrants, who could be arrested, fined, and hired out to white landowners. Some states limited the occupations open to blacks, and tried to prevent them from acquiring land. African-Americans strongly resisted the implementation of these measures, and the apparent inability of the South's white leaders to accept the reality of emancipation fatally undermined Northern support for Johnson's policies. The Black Codes, wrote one Republican, were attempts to "restore all of slavery but its name."

When Congress assembled in December 1865, Johnson announced that with loyal governments functioning in all the Southern states, Reconstruction was over. In response, Radical Republicans, who had grown increasingly estranged from Johnson during the summer and fall, called for the abrogation of these governments and the establishment of new ones with "rebels" excluded from power and black men granted the right to vote.

ANDREW JOHNSON

Andrew Johnson, seventeenth president of the United States, c. 1865. (Library of Congress)

The only president ever impeached and tried before the Senate, Andrew Johnson (1808–75) came from the humblest origins of any man who reached the White House. Born in poverty in North Carolina, he worked as a youth as a tailor's apprentice.

After moving to Greenville, Tennessee, Johnson achieved success through politics. Beginning as an alderman, he rose to serve two terms as governor. Although the owner of five slaves before the Civil War, Johnson identified himself as the champion of his state's "honest yeomen" and a foe of large planters, whom he described as a "bloated, corrupted aristocracy." He strongly promoted public education and free land for Western settlers.

A fervent believer in states' rights, Johnson was also a strong defender of the Union. He was the only senator from a seceding state to remain at his post in 1861, and when Union forces occupied Tennessee, Abraham Lincoln named him military governor. In 1864, he was elected vice president.

Succeeding to the presidency after Lincoln's death, Johnson failed to provide the nation with enlightened leadership and also failed to deal effectively with Congress. Racism prevented him from responding to black demands for civil rights and personal inflexibility rendered him unable to compromise with Congress. Johnson's vetoes of Reconstruction legislation and opposition to the Fourteenth Amendment alienated most Republicans. In 1868, he came within one vote of being removed from office by impeachment.

After leaving office in 1875, Johnson returned to Tennessee. He died shortly after being reelected to the Senate.

Andrew Johnson's Masonic apron, painted silk, c. 1860.
(Tennessee State Museum Collection)

In 1851, Andrew Johnson, then a U.S. Congressman, joined Masonic Lodge No. 3 in Greenville, Tennessee. Perhaps his lifelong devotion to the order reflected his aspirations to rise above his humble origins and the pride he took in doing so. The symbols on Johnson's ceremonial apron indicate that he had attained a high rank in the fraternal order.

Charles Sumner, U.S. senator from Massachusetts, c. 1865. (Chicago Historical Society)

Charles Sumner, an early opponent of slavery, advocate of equality before the law, and a leader of the Radical Repubicans, viewed Reconstruction as an opportunity to establish civil rights for African-Americans. He strongly opposed Andrew Johnson's Reconstruction policies and voted to convict the president at his impeachment trial in 1868. Sumner wrote the bill that became the Civil Rights Act of 1875, the final piece of Reconstruction legislation, which outlawed racial discrimination in transportation and places of public accommodation.

Most Republicans, however, were moderates, not Radicals. They believed Johnson's plan flawed, but desired to work with the president in modifying it and did not believe either Northern or Southern whites would accept black suffrage. Radicals and moderates joined together in refusing to seat the Southerners recently elected to Congress. Then they established a Joint Committee to investigate the progress of Reconstruction.

Early in 1866, Lyman Trumbull, a senator from Illinois, proposed two bills, reflecting the moderates' belief that Johnson's policy required modification. The first extended the life of the Freedmen's Bureau, which had been established for only one year. The second, the Civil Rights Bill, was described by one congressman as "one of the most important bills ever presented to the House for its action." This defined all persons born in the United States as citizens and spelled out rights they were to enjoy without regard to race—making contracts, bringing lawsuits, and enjoying "full and equal benefit of all laws and proceedings for the security of person and property." These, said Trumbull, were the "fundamental rights belonging to every man as a free man." The bill left the new Southern governments in place, but required them to accord blacks the same civil rights as whites. It made no mention of the right to vote. In effect, the bill voided the Black Codes, as well as numerous Northern laws discriminating against blacks, and the Supreme Court's Dred Scott decision of 1857, which had decreed that no African-American could be a citizen of the United States.

Passed by overwhelming majorities in both Houses of Congress, the Civil Rights Bill represented the first attempt to define in legislative terms the essence of freedom and the rights of American citizenship. In empowering the federal government to guarantee the principle of equality before the law, regardless of race, against violations by the states, it embodied a profound change in federal-state relations.

To the surprise of Congress, Johnson vetoed both bills. Both, he said, threatened to centralize power in the federal government and deprive the states of their authority to regulate their own affairs. Moreover, he believed blacks did not deserve the rights of citizenship. Johnson offered no possibility of compromising with Congress; he insisted instead that his own Reconstruction program be left unchanged. The vetoes made a complete breach between Congress and the president inevitable. In April 1866, the Civil Rights Bill became the first major law in American history to be passed over a presidential veto.

Unwittingly, Johnson had given cause for the moderate and Radical Republicans to unite against him. Congress now proceeded to adopt its own plan of Reconstruction. Its first task was to fix in the Constitution, beyond the reach of presidential vetoes and shifting electoral majorities, the Republican understanding of the legacy of the Civil War. In June, Congress approved the Fourteenth Amendment, which broadened the federal government's power to protect the rights of all Americans. It forbade states from abridging the "privileges and immunities" of American citizens or depriving any citizen of the "equal protection of the laws." In a compromise between Radical and moderate positions on black suffrage, it did not give blacks the right to vote, but threatened to reduce the South's representation in Congress if black men continued to be denied the ballot. The amendment also barred repayment of the Confederate debt and prohibited many Confederate leaders from holding state and national office. And it empowered Congress to take further steps to enforce the amendment's provisions.

The most important change in the Constitution since the adoption of the Bill of Rights, the Fourteenth Amendment established equality before the law as a fundamental right of American citizens. It shifted the balance of power within the nation by making the federal government, not the states, the ultimate protector of citizens' rights—a sharp departure from prewar traditions, which viewed centralized power, not local authority, as the basic threat to Americans' liberties. In authorizing future Congresses to define the meaning of equal rights, it made equality before the law a dynamic, elastic principle. In the twentieth century, many of the Supreme Court's most important decisions expanding the rights of American citizens have been based on the Fourteenth Amendment, perhaps most notably the 1954 ruling that outlawed school segregation.

Nonetheless, the amendment left some Republicans dissatisfied. Radicals like Pennsylvania Congressman Thaddeus Stevens and Senator Charles Sumner of Massachusetts were disappointed that it did not guarantee black suffrage. (The amendment, Stevens told the House, was a political compromise, but he supported it "because I live among men and not among angels.") The women's rights movement felt betrayed because in its representation section, the amendment for the first time introduced the word "male" into the Constitution. A state would lose representation if any men were denied the vote, but none if women continued to be disenfranchised.

The Fourteenth Amendment and the Congressional policy of guaranteeing civil rights for blacks became the central issues of the political campaign of 1866. Congress now demanded that in order the regain their seats in the House and Senate, the Southern states ratify the amendment. Johnson denounced the proposal and embarked on a speaking tour of the North, the "swing around the circle," to urge voters to elect congressmen committed to his own Reconstruction program. Denouncing his critics, the president made wild accusations that the Radicals were plotting to assassinate him. His behavior further undermined public support for his policies, as did riots that broke out in 1866 in Memphis and New Orleans, in which white policemen and citizens killed scores of blacks.

In the Northern congressional elections that fall, Republicans opposed to Johnson's policies won a sweeping victory. Nonetheless, egged on by Johnson, every Southern state but Tennessee refused to ratify the Fourteenth Amendment. Congress now moved to implement its own plan of Reconstruction. The intransigence of Johnson and the bulk of the white South pushed moderate

The Freedmen's Bureau, *campaign broadside, 1866.* (Library of Congress)

The national debate over Reconstruction, and in particular, the Freedmen's Bureau, is evident in a campaign broadside from Pennsylvania's gubernatorial campaign of 1866. The cartoon's racist imagery played upon public fears that government assistance would benefit indolent freedmen at the expense of white workers.

Republicans toward the proposals of the Radicals. In March 1867, over Johnson's veto, Congress adopted the Reconstruction Act, which divided the South into five military districts, temporarily barred many Confederates from voting or holding office, and called for the creation of new governments in the South, with black men given the right to vote. Only after the new governments ratified the Fourteenth Amendment could the Southern states finally be readmitted to the Union.

Thus began the period of Congressional or Radical Reconstruction, which lasted until the fall of the last Southern Republican government in 1877. It was

Burning a Freedman's Schoolhouse, *engraving based on a sketch*
by Alfred R. Waud, Harper's Weekly, May 26, 1866.

On May 1, 1866, two horsedrawn hacks, one driven by a black man, the other by a white man, acci-
dentally collided on a street in Memphis. When police arrested the black driver, a group of black vet-
erans recently discharged from the army intervened, and a white crowd began to gather. From this
incident followed three days of racial violence in which white mobs destroyed hundreds of structures in
the black community, including a freedman's school. At least forty-six blacks and two whites died in
the disturbance. The Memphis riot helped to discredit Andrew Johnson's Reconstruction policies by
indicating that many white Southerners did not accept the reality of emancipation.

the nation's first real experiment in interracial democracy. "We have cut loose
from the whole dead past," wrote one Republican senator, "and have cast our
anchor out a hundred years" into the future.

The conflict between President Johnson and Congress did not end with the
passage of the Reconstruction Act. In order to shield its policy against presidential interference, Congress in March 1867 adopted the Tenure of Office
Act, barring the president from removing certain officeholders, including Cab-
inet members, without the consent of the Senate. To Johnson, this was an
unconstitutional restriction of his authority. In February 1868, he removed
Secretary of War Edwin M. Stanton, an ally of the Radicals. The House of

President Andrew Johnson, lithograph by Currier & Ives, New York, 1868.
(Museum of American Political Life)

President Andrew Johnson's ability to work with Congress and his public popularity eroded as he followed a plan of Reconsturction that gave Southern whites a free hand in establishing new governments that threatened to reduce African-Americans to a condition similar to slavery. After Johnson vetoed several Reconstruction measures passed by Congress, his opponents charged him with autocratic behavior; one disgruntled citizen mocked the president by drawing a crown on his portrait.

Andrew Johnson's Reconstruction, *by Thomas Nast*, Harper's Weekly, *September 1, 1866.*

Nast's cartoon, casting President Johnson as Shakespeare's character Iago and a black Union soldier as Othello, reflects the North's anger over Andrew Johnson's Reconstruction policies. Johnson's vetoes of the Freedmen's Bureau and Civil Rights Bills, as well as his opposition to the Fourteenth Amendment, alienated most Republicans and eventually led to his impeachment in 1868.

Impeachment managers, 1868. (National Archives)

In March 1868, for the first time in American history, the U.S. House of Representatives voted to impeach an American president for "high crimes and misdemeanors." The House Board of Managers for the impeachment of Andrew Johnson included, standing from left to right: James F. Wilson, Iowa; George S. Boutwell, Massachusetts; John Logan, Illinois; and, seated, from left: Benjamin F. Butler, Massachusetts; Thaddeus Stevens, Pennsylvania; Thomas E. Williams, Pennsylvania; and John A. Bingham, Ohio.

Representatives responded by approving articles of impeachment against the president.

Thus, for the only time in American history, a president was placed on trial before the Senate for "high crimes and misdemeanors." If convicted of the charges against him, which essentially involved his violation of the Tenure of Office Act, Johnson would be removed from office. Virtually all Republicans, by this point, considered Johnson a failure as president and an obstacle to a lasting Reconstruction, but some moderates disliked the prospect of elevating to the presidency Benjamin Wade, a Radical who, as president pro tem of the Senate, would succeed Johnson. Others feared conviction would damage the constitutional separation of powers between Congress and the executive. The final tally was 35 to 19 to convict Johnson, one vote short of the two-thirds necessary to remove him from office. Seven Republicans had joined the Democrats in voting to acquit the president.

Formal Notice of the Impeachment of Andrew Johnson, *engraving from* **Frank Leslie's Illustrated Newspaper,** *March 14, 1868.*

On February 25, 1868, the House Managers of Impeachment, led by Thaddeus Stevens and John A. Bingham, went before the U.S. Senate to present eleven articles of impeachment against President Andrew Johnson. The case rested on Johnson's removal of Secretary of War Edwin M. Stanton from office, but in reality grew out of congressional disapproval of Johnson's Reconstruction policies. On May 26, 1868, the Senate voted 35 to 19 to convict Johnson, one vote short of the two-thirds necessary to remove him from office.

Johnson's acquittal weakened the Radicals' position within the party, and made the nomination of Ulysses S. Grant as the party's presidential candidate all but inevitable. As the nation's greatest war hero, Grant possessed obvious advantages as a candidate. After initially supporting Johnson's policies, Grant had come to side with Congress, but Radicals worried that he lacked strong ideological convictions. His Democratic opponent was Horatio Seymour, the colorless former governor of New York.

Reconstruction was the central issue of the 1868 campaign. The Republican platform declared black suffrage in the South essential for reasons of "public safety, of gratitude, and of justice," but failed to take a forthright position on whether Northern blacks should be allowed to vote. It did insist, however, that

Ulysses S. Grant, Mathew Brady Studio, Washington, D.C., c. 1868.
(Chicago Historical Society)

In 1868, Civil War hero Ulysses S. Grant ran as the Republican party's nominee for president and narrowly defeated his Democratic opponent Horatio Seymour, former governor of New York. Grant supported Republican Reconstruction policies but aligned himself with the moderate wing of the party. Despite the corruption that marked his first administration, Grant easily won reelection in 1872.

Congressional Reconstruction must go forward. Democrats denounced Reconstruction as unconstitutional and condemned black suffrage as a violation of America's political traditions. The campaign was bitter. Republicans identified their opponents with secession and treason, a tactic known as "waving the bloody shirt." Democrats appealed openly to racism, charging that Reconstruction would lead to interracial marriage and black supremacy throughout the nation.

Presidential campaign buttons, 1868. (Museum of American Political Life)

Ulysses S. Grant chose Schuyler Colfax, former Speaker of the House, as his running mate in the 1868 presidential campaign. "Let Us Have Peace," the last line of Grant's letter accepting the nomination, became the Republicans' campaign slogan. The Democrats' nominee, Horatio Seymour, ran on a platform opposing Reconstruction. "This Is a White Man's Government" became the slogan of a Democratic campaign that openly appealed to racial fears and prejudice.

Grant won the election, although by a margin many Republicans found uncomfortably close. He received overwhelming support from black voters in the South, but Seymour may well have carried a majority of the nation's white vote. Nonetheless, the result was a vindication of Republican Reconstruction and inspired Congress to adopt the era's third amendment to the constitution. In February 1869, Congress approved the Fifteenth Amendment, prohibiting the federal and state governments from depriving any citizen of the right to vote because of race. Bitterly opposed by the Democratic party, it became part of the Constitution in 1870.

Although it left the door open to suffrage restrictions not explicitly based on race—literacy tests, property qualifications, poll taxes—and did nothing to extend the right to vote to women, the Fifteenth Amendment marked the culmination of four decades of agitation on behalf of the slave. As late as 1868, even

This Is A White Man's Government, *by Thomas Nast,*
Harper's Weekly, *September 5, 1868.*

During the 1868 presidential campaign, political cartoonist Thomas Nast ridiculed the Democratic party as a coalition of Irish immigrants (left), white supremacists like Nathan Bedford Forrest, leader of the Ku Klux Klan (center), and Northern capitalists represented by Horatio Seymour, the presidential nominee (right). Nast's cartoon depicted Democrats as the oppressors of the black race, represented by a black Union soldier felled while carrying the American flag and a ballot box.

after Congress had enfranchised black men in the South, only eight Northern states had allowed black men to vote. In March 1870, the American Anti-Slavery Society disbanded, its work, its members believed, now complete. "Nothing in all history," exclaimed veteran abolitionist William Lloyd Garrison, equaled "this wonderful, quiet, sudden transformation of four millions of human beings from . . . the auction-block to the ballot-box."

Congressional Reconstruction policy was now essentially complete. Henceforth, the focus of Reconstruction lay within the South.

THADDEUS STEVENS

*Thaddeus Stevens, congressman from
Pennsylvania and leader of the Radical
Republicans, c. 1865.* (Library of Congress)

The most prominent Radical Republican in Congress during Reconstruction, Thaddeus Stevens (1792–1868) was born and educated in New England. He moved as a young man to Pennsylvania, where he practiced law, became an iron manufacturer, and entered politics.

Stevens served several terms in the legislature, where he won renown as an advocate of free public education. He also championed the rights of Pennsylvania's black population. A delegate to the constitutional convention of 1838, he refused to sign the document because it limited voting to whites.

As a congressman, Stevens during the Civil War urged the administration to free and arm the slaves and by 1865 favored black suffrage in the South. He became one of Andrew Johnson's fiercest critics and an early advocate of his impeachment.

To Stevens, Reconstruction offered an opportunity to create a "perfect republic" based on the principle of equal rights for all citizens. As floor leader of House Republicans, he helped to shepherd Reconstruction legislation through Congress, although he thought much of it too moderate. His plan for confiscating the land of Confederate planters and dividing it among Northern settlers and the former slaves failed to pass.

After his death, Stevens was buried in an integrated cemetery in Pennsylvania, to illustrate, as the epitaph he had composed stated, "the principle which I advocated through a long life, Equality of Man before his Creator."

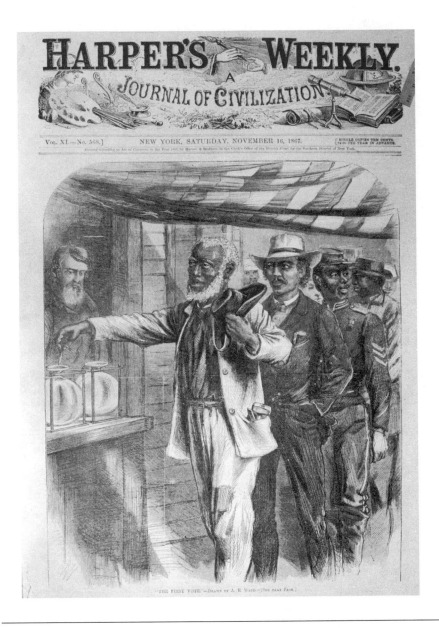

HARPER'S WEEKLY.

JOURNAL OF CIVILIZATION.

Vol. XI.—No. 568.]   NEW YORK, SATURDAY, NOVEMBER 16, 1867.   [SINGLE COPIES TEN CENTS.
[$4.00 PER YEAR IN ADVANCE.

The First Vote, *engraving based on a sketch by Alfred R. Waud,*
Harper's Weekly, *November 16, 1867.*

Under provisions of the Reconstruction Act passed by Congress in 1867, Southern states could no longer restrict the right to vote because of race. Thus, Southern black men could vote three years before the ratification of the Fifteenth Amendment, which enfranchised American black men throughout the nation. Waud's engraving depicts three members of the black community—an artisan, a member of the middle class, and a soldier—standing in line to cast their ballots.

Reconstruction Government in the South

Among the former slaves, the passage of the Reconstruction Act of 1867, which brought black suffrage to the South, caused an outburst of political organization. Determined to exercise their new rights as citizens, thousands joined the Union League, an organization closely linked to the Republican party, and the vast majority of eligible African-Americans registered to vote. "You never saw a people more excited on the subject of politics than are the Negroes of the South," wrote a plantation manager.

By 1870, all the former Confederate states had met the requirements of Congress and been readmitted to the Union, and nearly all were under the control of the Republican party. Their new constitutions, drafted in 1868 and 1869 by the first public bodies in American history with substantial black representation (of about 1,000 delegates throughout the South, over one-quarter were black), represented a considerable improvement over those they replaced. They made the structure of Southern government more democratic, modernized the tax system, and guaranteed the civil and political rights of black citizens. A few states initially barred former Confederates from voting, but this policy was quickly abandoned by the new state governments.

Throughout Reconstruction, black voters provided the bulk of the Republican party's support. Although Democrats charged that "Negro rule" had come to the South, nowhere did blacks control the workings of state government, and nowhere did they hold office in numbers equal to their proportion of the total population (which ranged from about 60 percent in South Carolina to around one-third in Arkansas, North Carolina, Tennessee, and Texas). Nonetheless, the fact that well over 1,500 African-Americans occupied positions of political power in the Reconstruction South represented a stunning departure in American government.

Election campaign in Baton Rouge, Louisiana, c.1868.
(Andrew D. Lytle Collection, Louisiana and Lower Mississippi Valley Collections,
LSU Libraries, Louisiana State University)

American politics followed its noisy tradition in the South during Reconstruction with rallies, parades, and the ubiquitous brass band. The Union League, a Republican organization, conducted many campaigns and registered thousands of voters for local, state, and national elections.

During Reconstruction, blacks were represented at every level of government. Fourteen sat in the House of Representatives, and two, Hiram Revels and Blanche K. Bruce, represented Mississippi in the Senate. P. B. S. Pinchback of Louisiana served briefly as America's first black governor (a century and a quarter would pass until C. Douglas Wilder of Virginia, elected in 1989, became the second). Other blacks held major state executive positions, including lieutenant governor, treasurer, and superintendent of education. Nearly 700 sat in state legislatures during Reconstruction, and there were scores of black local officials, ranging from justice of the peace to sheriff, tax assessor, and policeman. The presence of black officeholders and their white allies made a real difference

The State Convention at Richmond, Virginia in Session, *engraving,*
Frank Leslie's Illustrated Newspaper, *February 15, 1868.*

The Reconstruction Act of 1867 stipulated that all former Confederate states except Tennessee hold conventions to draft new constitutions. In 1868–69, 265 black delegates, or one-quarter of the total, attended these conventions, making them the first public bodies in American history with substantial black representation. In Virginia, blacks made up one-fifth of the convention.

in Southern life, ensuring that those accused of crimes would be tried before juries of their peers, and enforcing fairness in such prosaic aspects of local government as road repair, tax assessment, and poor relief.

Many of these officeholders had been born free, and around fifty had gained their liberty before the Civil War, by manumission, purchase, or escape. In South Carolina and Louisiana, homes of the South's wealthiest and best-educated free black communities, most prominent Reconstruction officeholders had never experienced slavery. A number of black Reconstruction officials had come from the North after the Civil War. The majority, however, were former slaves who had established their leadership in the black community by serving

ROBERT B. ELLIOTT

*Robert B. Elliott, congressman from
South Carolina.* (Library of Congress)

One of the South's most brilliant political organizers during Reconstruction, Robert B. Elliott (1842–84) appears to have been born in Liverpool, England, of West Indian parents, and to have come to Boston on a British naval vessel shortly after the Civil War.

After moving to South Carolina in 1867, Elliott established a law practice and helped to organize the Republican party. He "knew the political condition of every nook and corner throughout the state," said one political ally. Elliott served in the constitutional convention of 1868 and the state legislature, and was twice elected to Congress. He resigned in 1874 to fight political corruption

in South Carolina, where he became Speaker of the House.

In Congress, Elliott delivered a celebrated speech in favor of the bill that became the Civil Rights Act of 1875, which prohibited discrimination because of race in public accommodations. Elliott himself had been denied service in a restaurant while traveling to Washington.

In 1881, Elliott headed a delegation that met with president-elect James A. Garfield to complain that with the end of Reconstruction, Southern blacks were "citizens in name and not in fact." Because of his role in politics, Elliott's law practice was boycotted by white clients. He died penniless in New Orleans.

THE FIRST COLORED SENATOR AND REPRESENTATIVES.

In the 41st and 42nd Congress of the United States.

The First Colored Senator and Representatives,
lithograph, Currier & Ives, 1872. (Library of Congress)

The Forty-first and Forty-second Congress included black members for the first time in American history. A commemorative print issued at the time portrays Senator Hiram Revels of Mississippi, and representatives Robert DeLarge of South Carolina, Jefferson Long of Georgia, Benjamin Turner of Alabama, Josiah Walls of Florida, and Joseph Rainey and Robert B. Elliott of South Carolina. A total of sixteen blacks sat in Congress during Reconstruction.

in the Union army, working as ministers, teachers, or skilled craftsmen, or engaging in Union League organizing. The son of Emanuel Fortune, a Florida lawmaker, explained how his father's Reconstruction prominence had its roots before the Civil War: "It was natural from him to take the leadership in any independent movement of the Negroes. . . . In such life as the slaves were allowed and in church work, he took the leader's part. When the matter of the Constitutional Convention was decided upon his people in Jackson County naturally looked to him to shape up matters for them."

Hiram Revels and Blanche K. Bruce

Portrait of Hiram Revels, by Theodor Kaufmann, oil on canvas, c. 1870. (Herbert F. Johnson Museum of Art, Cornell University)

Blanche K. Bruce, senator from Mississippi. (Library of Congress)

The first African-Americans to serve in the United States Senate, Hiram R. Revels (1822–1901) and Blanche K. Bruce (1841–98) illustrate the diverse backgrounds and community activities of Reconstruction's black political leaders.

Revels was born free in North Carolina, attended Knox College in Illinois, and before the Civil War preached throughout the Midwest for the African Methodist Episcopal church. During the Civil War, he served as chaplain for a black regiment. Revels went to Mississippi in 1865 and became involved in the movement to establish schools for the former slaves.

After being elected to the state Senate in 1869, Revels was chosen by the legislature to fill Mississippi's unexpired term in the U.S. Senate, serving from February 1870 to March 1871. After leaving the Senate, Revels was for several years president of Alcorn University, an institution for African-American students established during Reconstruction. He also worked for the Methodist Episcopal Church, which he had joined during the Civil War, and in 1876 unsuccessfully protested his church's plans to hold racially segregated annual conferences in the South.

Blanche K. Bruce was born a slave. He may have been the son of his owner, a wealthy Virginia planter, and was educated by the same private tutor who instructed his master's legitimate child. Bruce was taken to Missouri in 1850, and in the early days of the Civil War escaped to Kansas, where he established the state's first school for African-American children.

Bruce went to Mississippi in 1868 with seventy-five cents to his name and launched a successful political career in Bolivar county, where he served as sheriff and tax collector, and edited a local newspaper. During his term in the Senate (1875–81), he worked to obtain federal aid for economic development in Mississippi. A staunch defender of black civil rights, Bruce also spoke eloquently in opposition to the 1878 law prohibiting Chinese immigrants from entering the United States.

Bruce remained in Washington after his term expired, holding a succession of government appointments. His wife, Josephine, who had been the first black teacher in the Cleveland public schools, went on to serve as Woman Principal of Tuskegee Institute in Alabama.

Louisiana Constitution and Members of Convention, *1868*. (Library of Congress)

Blacks, most of them freeborn, formed a majority of delegates at the Louisiana Constitutional Convention of 1868. They included Oscar J. Dunn, the state's lieutenant governor, and P. B. S. Pinchback, who became lieutenant governor and subsequently governor. Like all new Southern constitutions written after the war, Louisiana's guaranteed blacks civil and political rights.

PINCKNEY B. S. PINCHBACK

P. B. S. Pinchback, lieutenant governor and governor of Louisiana. (Library of Congress)

The only African-American to serve as governor of a state until the election of Virginia's C. Douglas Wilder in 1989, Pinckney B. S. Pinchback (1837–1921) exemplified the combination of motives, including desire for reform and an eye for personal gain, that inspired many Reconstruction leaders.

Born in Georgia, the son of a white planter and a free African-American woman, Pinchback attended school in Cincinnati and worked as a steward on Mississippi River steamboats. He made his way to New Orleans in 1862 and was appointed to recruit black soldiers for the Union army. He resigned from the army in 1863 after encountering discrimination from white officers.

As early as November 1863, Pinchback spoke at a rally in New Orleans demanding voting rights for blacks. He served in the constitutional convention of 1868, where he wrote the provision guaranteeing all citizens equal treatment in transportation and by businesses. Elected lieutenant governor in 1871, Pinchback became governor when Henry C. Warmoth was impeached in December 1872, serving for five weeks.

Pinchback accumulated considerable wealth while in office during Reconstruction, partly through a mercantile business he operated with another black lawmaker and partly through speculation in state bonds, the sale of real estate to the government at inflated prices, and other corrupt means. He remained a power in Louisiana politics into the 1890s.

MIFFLIN GIBBS AND JONATHAN GIBBS

Mifflin Gibbs, attorney and judge, Arkansas. (Schomburg Center for Research in Black Culture)

Jonathan Gibbs, secretary of state and superintendant of education in Florida. (Moorland-Spingarn Research Center, Howard University)

The sons of an African-American minister in Philadelphia, Mifflin Gibbs (1823–1915) and Jonathan Gibbs (1827–74) had remarkable careers before becoming involved in Reconstruction politics.

A building contractor active in the antislavery movement, Mifflin Gibbs left Philadelphia for California in 1850 to take part in the gold rush. In 1855, he founded the state's first black newspaper, which campaigned for granting California's blacks the right to vote. Three years later, Gibbs moved to British Columbia, where he became involved in mining and railroad ventures and was twice elected to the Victoria city council.

Gibbs returned to the United States after the Civil War, studied at Oberlin College, and in 1871 moved to Arkansas, where he served as a judge in Little Rock. As an attorney, he won a case against a saloon that refused to serve black patrons. Gibbs remained active in Republican politics into the twentieth century, and from 1897 to 1901 was U.S. consul at Madagascar. In 1902, he published his autobiography, *Shadow and Light.*

Jonathan Gibbs was educated in Philadelphia and then, he later related, was "refused admittance into eighteen colleges because of my color." Eventually, he attended Dartmouth College, graduating in 1852. He then served as a Presbyterian minister in New York and Pennsylvania.

Sent to North Carolina as a religious missionary after the Civil War, Gibbs opened a school for the freedpeople, and then moved to Florida. He was appointed Secretary of State in 1868, and Superintendent of Education in 1873, becoming the only African-American to hold statewide office in Florida during Reconstruction. Hoping to counteract Democratic charges that blacks were by nature incapable of taking part in government, he wrote sketches of "distinguished colored men," past and present, for a local newspaper.

The new Southern Republican party also brought to power whites who had enjoyed little authority before the Civil War. Many Reconstruction officials were Northerners who for one reason or another had migrated South during and after the war. Their opponents dubbed them "carpetbaggers," implying that they had packed all their belongings in a suitcase and left their homes, in order to reap the spoils of office in the South. Some carpetbaggers were undoubtedly corrupt adventurers. The large majority, however, were former Union soldiers who decided to remain in the South when the war ended, before there was any prospect of going into politics. Others were investors in land and railroads who saw in the postwar South an opportunity to combine personal economic advancement with a role in helping mold the "backward" South in the image of the modern, industrializing North, substituting, as one wrote, "the civilization of freedom for that of slavery." Still another large group of carpetbaggers were teachers, Freedmen's Bureau officers, and others who came to the region genuinely hoping to assist the former slaves.

The largest group of white Republicans had been born in the South. Former Confederates reserved their greatest scorn for these "scalawags," whom they considered traitors to their race and region. Some were men of stature and wealth, such as James L. Alcorn, a former Whig leader and Mississippi's first Republican governor. Others were business entrepreneurs who believed a "new era" had dawned in the South, and that the Republican party was more likely to promote economic development than the Democratic. The largest number of scalawags, however, were nonslaveholding white farmers from the Southern upcountry. Some had been wartime Unionists who cooperated with the Republicans in order to prevent Rebels from returning to power. Unionists, declared a North Carolina Republican newspaper, must choose "between salvation at the hand of the Negro or destruction at the hand of the rebel." Other scalawags hoped Reconstruction governments would help them recover from wartime economic losses by suspending the collection of debts and enacting laws protecting small property holders from losing their homes to creditors. Nowhere in the South during Reconstruction did the Republican party receive a majority of the white vote, but in states like North Carolina, Tennessee, and Arkansas, it initially commanded a significant minority.

Given the fact that many of the Reconstruction governors and legislators lacked previous experience in government, their record of accomplishment is remarkable. In many ways, Reconstruction at the state level greatly expanded the scope of public responsibility in the South. The new governments established the region's first state-supported public school systems, as well as numerous hospitals and asylums for orphans and the insane. These institutions were open to black

ROBERT SMALLS

*Robert Smalls, Civil War hero
and congressman from South Carolina.*
(Library of Congress)

Among the most celebrated black heroes of the Civil War, Robert Smalls (1839–1915) had a political career that stretched into the twentieth century.

Born a slave in Beaufort, South Carolina, Smalls worked on the Charleston docks before the Civil War. Employed by the Confederacy as a pilot on the *Planter,* Smalls secretly guided the ship out of Charleston harbor in May 1862 and delivered it to federal forces. He was given a reward of $1,500 and made a second lieutenant in the Union navy. In 1864, Smalls was evicted from a segregated Philadelphia streetcar; a mass protest followed that led to the integration of the city's public transportation.

During Reconstruction, Smalls became a powerful political leader on the South Carolina Sea Islands. He represented Beaufort in the constitutional convention of 1868, published a local newspaper, and was elected to five terms in Congress. In 1895, he was one of six black delegates to the state constitutional convention, where he protested against the decision to deprive blacks of the right to vote. Until 1913, he held office as collector of customs at Beaufort.

Reconstruction of the South, *lithograph by John Smith, Philadelphia, c. 1870.*
(National Museum of American History, Smithsonian Institution)

An optimistic view of Reconstruction with Biblical overtones presents key elements of the Republican plan to remake the South. The central figure is George Peabody, whose philanthropy supported Southern schools but opposed racial integration. On either side are Union Army officers transforming military weapons into tools for agriculture. In the background "300,000" mechanics, backed by northern capital, carry tools for the "Reconstruction of the Union."

and white Southerners, although generally, they were segregated by race. Only in New Orleans were the public schools integrated during Reconstruction, and only in South Carolina did the state university admit black students (elsewhere separate colleges were established for blacks). By the 1870s, in a region whose prewar leaders had made it illegal for blacks to learn and had done little to promote education among poorer whites, over half the children were attending public schools.

In assuming public responsibility for education, Reconstruction governments in a sense were following a path blazed by the North. Their efforts to guarantee African-Americans equal treatment in transportation and places of public accommodation, however, launched these governments into an area all but unknown in American law. Racial segregation, or the complete exclusion of

JAMES L. ALCORN

James L. Alcorn, governor of Mississippi.
(Library of Congress)

Born in Illinois but raised in Kentucky, James L. Alcorn (1816–94) became Mississippi's first Reconstruction governor, and perhaps the era's most prominent "scalawag," or Southern white Republican.

In 1844 Alcorn moved to Mississippi, where he married a planter's daughter, and became one of the largest landowners in the Yazoo-Mississippi Delta. In 1860, he strongly opposed secession. After serving briefly in the Confederate army, Alcorn retired to his plantation.

At the end of the Civil War, Alcorn broke with his state's political leadership by advocating limited black suffrage and supporting the Fourteenth Amendment. In 1867, he joined the Republican party, insisting that only if men like himself took the lead in Reconstruction could a "harnessed revolu-

tion" take place. Blacks' rights would be respected, but political power would remain in white hands.

Elected governor in 1869, Alcorn appointed many white Democrats to office and opposed civil rights legislation. Black leaders and carpetbaggers became disaffected from his administration. Alcorn resigned in 1871 to take a seat in the U.S. Senate. Two years later, alarmed by blacks' increasing political assertiveness, he again ran for governor, this time with Democratic support. He was defeated by Adelbert Ames.

After Reconstruction, Alcorn remained a Republican. But as a delegate to the constitutional convention of 1890, he supported the clause taking the right to vote away from Mississippi blacks, perhaps hoping to restore white domination of his party.

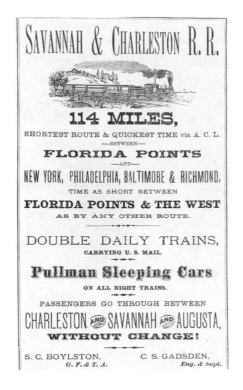

*Advertisement for the Savannah and Charleston Railroad from
the Charleston City Directory, 1878.* (**South Carolina Historical Society**)

*Reconstruction governments of the South believed that the development of a regional railroad system
with links to Northern markets would create a more diversified economy with opportunites for blacks
and whites alike. Although thousands of miles of track were laid during Reconstruction, the program
never realized its goals, partly because Northern investors preferred economic opportunities in the West.*

blacks from both public and private facilities, was widespread throughout the
country. Black demands for the outlawing of such discrimination produced deep
divisions in the Republican party. But in the Deep South, where blacks made up
the vast majority of the Republican voting population, laws were enacted
making it illegal for railroads, hotels, and other institutions to discriminate on
the basis of race. Enforcement of these laws varied considerably from locality to
locality, but Reconstruction established for the first time at the state level a
standard of equal citizenship and a recognition of blacks' right to a share of
public services.

Republican governments also took steps to assist the poor of both races and to promote the South's economic recovery. The Black Codes were repealed, the property of small farmers protected against being seized for debt, and the tax system revised to shift the burden from propertyless blacks, who had paid a disproportionate share during Presidential Reconstruction, to planters and other landowners. The former slaves, however, were disappointed that little was done to assist them in acquiring land. Only South Carolina took effective action, establishing a commission to purchase land for resale on long-term credit to poor families.

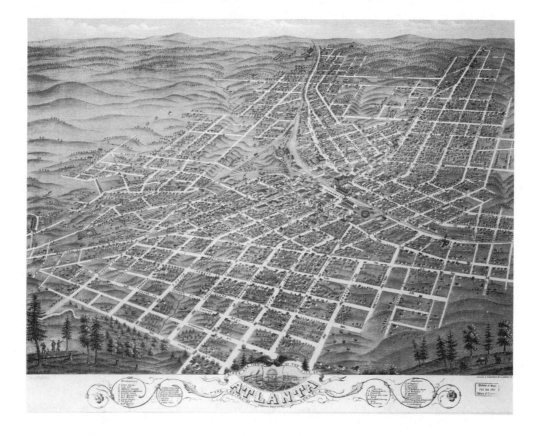

Bird's-Eye View of the City of Atlanta, *lithograph by A. Ruger, 1871.*
(Library of Congress)

Atlanta, captured and burned by Union troops in 1864, rebuilt itself after the Civil War. Located at the juncture of several railroad lines, the city attracted new businesses, and its population tripled to about 21,000 people by 1870. Adding to its status, Atlanta became the state capital in 1868.

SIMEON CORLEY

***Simeon Corley, congressman from
South Carolina.*** **(Library of Congress)**

Born in South Carolina, Simeon Corley (1823–1902) exemplified the connection among some white Southerners between prewar Unionism, hostility to the planter elite, and support for Reconstruction.

Before the Civil War, Corley worked as a tailor and wrote columns for the *Southern Patriot,* in which he opposed disunion and supported the temperance movement. As he later recalled, he was "hated and despised" for his views, and demands were raised that he be expelled from the state. Nonetheless, in 1863, he was drafted into the Confederate army.

Corley opposed Andrew Johnson's Recon- struction policies for placing the South "again under the rule of . . . traitors." Appealing to voters as a representative of "the great laboring class," white and black, he was elected as a Republican to the constitu- tional convention of 1868, a term in Con- gress, and a number of local offices. Ordinary South Carolinians, he declared, should rejoice at the death of slavery, "that great curse to both races," and the removal from power of the state's old political leaders.

Corley held no further positions after the end of Reconstruction, but lived for the remainder of his life in his native state.

ADELBERT AMES

Adelbert Ames, governor of Mississippi.
(Library of Congress)

A native of Maine, Adelbert Ames (1835–1933) graduated in 1861 from the U.S. Military Academy at West Point. He served with distinction in the Union Army, winning the Congressional Medal of Honor for bravery at the Battle of Bull Run.

Appointed by President Grant to command the fourth military district (including Mississippi) under the Reconstruction Act of 1867, Ames became convinced that he "had a Mission with a large M" to assist the former slaves. He appointed blacks to local offices and ordered that, for the first time in the state's history, they be eligible to serve on juries.

Elected to the U.S. Senate in 1870, Ames became leader of the Republican faction that opposed the moderate policies of

Gov. James L. Alcorn. In 1873, black leaders urged Ames to run for governor, and he handily defeated Alcorn. As governor, Ames attempted to reduce the cost of government and make public land available to the former slaves.

In 1875, Democrats launched a violent campaign to win control of the Mississippi legislature. Ames appealed for federal intervention to restore order, but without success.

After the Democratic victory, Ames resigned as governor, returned to the North, and went into his father's flour-milling business. For the remainder of his life, he continued to defend his Reconstruction record, insisting that racial discrimination was "the curse of the world."

Rather than land distribution, the Reconstruction governments pinned their hopes for Southern economic growth and opportunity for African-Americans on a program of regional economic development. Railroad construction was its centerpiece, the key, they believed, to linking the South with Northern markets, and transforming the region into a society of booming factories, bustling towns, and diversified agriculture. "A free and living Republic," declared a Tennessee Republican, would "spring up in the track of the railroad." The plantation would lose its dominant role in the economy, and new opportunities for employment and the acquisition of property would emerge for black and white alike. Every state during Reconstruction helped to finance railroad construction, and through tax reductions and other incentives, tried to attract Northern manufacturers to invest in the region. The program had mixed results. A few states—Georgia, Alabama, Arkansas, and Texas—witnessed significant new railroad construction between 1868 and 1872, but economic development in general remained weak. With abundant opportunities existing in the West, few Northern investors ventured to the Reconstruction South.

Thus, to their supporters, the governments of Radical Reconstruction presented a complex pattern of achievement and disappointment. The economic vision of a modernizing, revitalized Southern economy failed to materialize, and most African-Americans remained locked in poverty. On the other hand, biracial democratic government, a thing unknown in American history, for the first time functioned effectively in many parts of the South. Public facilities were rebuilt and expanded, school systems established, and legal codes purged of racism. The conservative oligarchy that had dominated Southern government from colonial times to 1867 found itself largely excluded from political power, while those who had previously been outsiders—poorer white Southerners, men from the North, and especially former slaves—cast ballots, sat on juries, and enacted and administered laws. The effect upon African-Americans was strikingly visible. "One hardly realizes the fact that the many Negroes one sees here . . . ," a Northern correspondent reported in 1873, "have been slaves a few short years ago, at least as far as their demeanor goes as individuals newly invested with all the rights and privileges of an American citizen."

The South's traditional leaders—planters, merchants, and Democratic politicians—bitterly opposed the new Southern governments, denouncing them as corrupt, inefficient, and embodiments of wartime defeat and "black supremacy." There was corruption during Reconstruction, but it was confined to no race, region, or party. Frauds that existed in some Southern states, associated primarily with the new programs of railroad aid, were dwarfed by those practiced

Murder of Louisiana, *by A. Zenneck, 1873.* **(Library of Congress)**

A cartoon opposing Reconstruction depicts President Ulysses S. Grant preparing to sacrifice the state of Louisiana on the "Altar of Radicalism." The devil, represented by Attorney General George H. Williams, directs Grant. The victim, held by two black men, has already had his heart removed by Louisiana's Republican governor William P. Kellogg. Northern merchants and Southern states, led by South Carolina wrapped in chains, witness the event from either side.

in these years by the Whiskey Rings, which involved high officials of the Grant administration, and by New York's Tweed Ring, controlled by the Democrats, whose depredations ran into the tens of millions of dollars.

The rising taxes needed to pay for schools and other new public facilities, and to assist railroad development, were another cause of opposition to Reconstruction. Planters resented the new tax systems, which forced them to bear a far higher share of the tax burden than in the past. Many poorer whites who had initially supported the Republican party turned against it when it became clear that their economic situation was not improving under the new governments.

The Black Vomit; Or, the Bottom Rail on Top, *broadside, c. 1870.* (Library of Congress)

Shortly after Republicans gained control of state governments in the South, Democrats launced a wide-spread campain to oust them. A broadside from Virginia illustrates the extent to which they used racism as a political tool. "Bottom Rail on Top" refers to a phrase coined by a former slave describing the status of black Americans after the Civil War. Democrats regained full control of Virginia in 1873.

The most basic reason for opposition to Reconstruction, however, was that most white Southerners could not accept the idea of former slaves voting, holding office, and enjoying equality before the law. They had always regarded blacks as an inferior race whose proper place was as dependent laborers. Reconstruction, they believed, had to be overthrown in order to restore white supremacy in Southern government, and to ensure planters a disciplined, reliable labor force. Even Southern Democrats like Benjamin H. Hill of Georgia,

Benjamin H. Hill, engraving by Illman Brothers Engravers, c. 1870.
(University of Georgia)

Benjamin Hill, a planter, lawyer, and legislator from Georgia, became spokesman for the New Departure, a movement among Democrats to regain political control of the South. Hill claimed to have a moderate approach to racial issues, and advocated a mixed economy of small farms, diversified agriculture, and modern industry. Hill believed that only the South's traditional leadership could enact such programs, not blacks, scalawags, or carpetbaggers.

who believed the Civil War had demonstrated "the superiority of Yankee civilization," and who accepted the premise that the South must move from a plantation-oriented economy to one of small farms and developing industry, insisted that such policies could only be carried out by the region's traditional leaders, not blacks, carpetbaggers, and scalawags.

In 1869 and 1870, Democrats joined with dissident Republicans to win control of Tennessee and Virginia, effectively ending Reconstruction there. Elsewhere in the South, however, with Reconstruction governments securely entrenched, their opponents turned to a campaign of widespread violence in an effort to end Republican rule. Their actions soon posed a fundamental challenge both for Reconstruction governments in the South and for policymakers in Washington.

ALBION W. TOURGÉE

Albion W. Tourgée, North Carolina jurist.
(Library of Congress)

Throughout his long career, carpetbagger Albion W. Tourgée (1838–1905) advocated equal rights for African-Americans. Born on an Ohio farm, he attended the University of Rochester before serving in the Union Army. He was twice wounded and spent four months in Confederate prisons.

After the war, Tourgée moved with his wife to North Carolina, where he became involved in Reconstruction politics. At the constitutional convention of 1868, he was instrumental in democratizing the state's local government and judicial system.

As a superior court judge during Reconstruction, Tourgée courageously challenged the Ku Klux Klan. His appeals to Congress revealing the extent of violence helped speed passage of laws authorizing the use of troops against the Klan.

After 1877, Tourgée returned to the North, where he expressed his disappointment over the failure of Reconstruction in *A Fool's Errand,* a partly autobiographical account of a young carpetbagger's career. The book became a bestseller, and Tourgée wrote several other popular novels.

In 1896, Tourgée served without fee as attorney for Homer A. Plessy, who challenged a Louisiana law requiring the racial segregation of railroad cars. By denying blacks equal protection of the law, Tourgée argued, segregation violated the Fourteenth Amendment. In *Plessy v. Ferguson,* the Supreme Court upheld the law and announced the principle of "separate but equal." Not until 1954, in the *Brown v. Board of Education* school segregation decision, did the Court adopt Tourgée's earlier reasoning.

Tourgée spent his last years serving as U.S. consul at Bordeaux, France, were he died.

HENRY C. WARMOTH

Henry C. Warmoth, governor of Louisiana.
(Library of Congress)

The career of Henry C. Warmoth (1842–1931), Louisiana's first Republican governor, illustrates some of the less attractive features of Reconstruction politics.

A native of Illinois, Warmoth was working as a lawyer in Missouri when the Civil War began. He joined the Union Army in 1862 and went to Louisiana two years later as judge of the provost court. Warmoth quickly plunged into politics and was active in the formation of the state's Republican party.

In 1868, at the youthful age of twenty-six, Warmoth was elected governor and was reelected in 1870. His term in office was marked by intense party factionalism, caused by differences over policy (Warmoth opposed civil rights legislation and appointed Democrats to office), and battles between blacks and whites, and Northern- and Southern-born Republicans, for governmental positions. Corruption became widespread, and Warmoth himself received bribes from railroad companies seeking state aid.

In 1872, Warmoth joined the Liberal Republicans and supported Horace Greeley for President. After Greeley's defeat, Warmoth was impeached and suspended from office. His black lieutenant governor, P. B. S. Pinchback, replaced him.

Warmoth remained in Louisiana for the rest of his life, serving as collector of customs at New Orleans, 1890–93, and operating a successful sugar plantation.

A Prospective Scene in the "City of Oaks," *woodcut cartoon by Ryland Randolph,*
Independent Monitor, *Tuscaloosa, Alabama, September 1, 1868.*

This cartoon sent a threat to a carpetbagger from Ohio, the Rev. A. S. Lakin, who had just been elected president of the University of Alabama, and Dr. N. B. Cloud, a scalawag serving as Superintendent of Public Instruction of Alabama. The Klan succeeded in driving both men from their positions.

The Ending of Reconstruction

The Civil War ended in 1865, but violence remained endemic in large parts of the postwar South. Although conflicts between white Unionists and Confederates contributed to the unsettled condition of life, in the vast majority of cases, former slaves were the victims and Southern whites the aggressors. In the early years of Reconstruction, violence was mostly local and unorganized—a reflection of individual whites' determination to define in their own way the meaning of freedom, and their resistance to blacks' efforts to establish their own autonomy. Freedpeople were assaulted and murdered for refusing to give way to whites on city sidewalks, using "insolent" language, or sending their children to school. Probably the largest number of violent acts in 1865 and 1866 stemmed from disputes over the control of labor. The victims included blacks who attempted to leave plantations, challenged contract settlements, or attempted to buy land.

The violence that greeted the advent of Republican governments after 1867, however, was far more pervasive, more organized, and more explicitly motivated by politics. In wide areas of the South, Reconstruction's opponents resorted to terror to secure their aim of restoring Democratic rule and white supremacy. Secret societies sprang up whose purpose was to prevent blacks from voting, and to destroy the infrastructure of the Republican party by assassinating local leaders and public officials.

The most notorious such organization was the Ku Klux Klan, which in effect served as a military arm of the Democratic party. Founded in 1866 as a Tennessee social club, the Klan was soon transformed into an organization of terrorist criminals, which spread into nearly every Southern state. Led by planters, merchants, and Democratic politicians, men who liked to style themselves the

John B. Gordon. (Library of Congress)

Georgia rice planter, Confederate general, and Democratic candidate for governor in 1868, John B. Gordon headed the Ku Klux Klan in his native state. The Klan, founded in 1866 as a social club in Tennessee, became a loosely organized group of white supremacists who waged local campaigns of violence and terror against blacks and white Republicans throughout the South.

South's "respectable citizens" and "natural rulers," the Klan committed some of the most brutal acts of violence in American history. During the 1868 presidential election, Klansmen assassinated Arkansas congressman James M. Hinds, three members of the South Carolina legislature, and other Republican leaders. In Georgia and Louisiana, the Klan established a reign of terror so complete that blacks were unable to go to the polls to vote, and Democrats carried both states for Horatio Seymour.

Grant's election did not end the Klan's activities; indeed in some parts of the South, Klan violence accelerated in 1869 and 1870. The Klan singled out for assault Reconstruction's local leadership. White Republicans—local office-holders, teachers, and party organizers—were often victimized. In 1870 William Luke, an Irish-born teacher in a black school, was lynched in Alabama along with four black men. Female teachers were beaten as well as male.

Nathan Bedford Forrest. **(Civil War Photographic Album, Louisiana and Lower Mississippi Valley Collections, LSU Libraries, Louisiana State University)**

Responsible for the Fort Pillow Massacre in which Confederate troops murdered black Union soldiers after they had surrendered, Lt. General Nathan B. Forrest of the Confederate cavalry later served as Grand Wizard of the Ku Klux Klan. The Klan, which served the interests of the Democratic party, included many prominent members of Southern society as well as middle-class and poor whites.

African-Americans, however, especially local leaders, bore the brunt of Klan violence. In Georgia, Klansmen in 1869 forced black legislator Abram Colby into the woods "and there stripped and beat him in the most cruel manner for nearly three hours." One black leader in Monroe County, Mississippi, had his throat cut because he was "president of a republican club" and was known as a man who "would speak his mind." In York County, South Carolina, where nearly the entire white male population joined the Klan (and women participated by sewing the robes Klansmen wore as disguises), the organization committed eleven murders and hundreds of whippings. By early 1871, thousands of blacks hid out in the woods each night to avoid assault.

Occasionally, violence escalated from attacks on individuals to wholesale assaults on the local African-American community. Institutions like black churches and schools, symbols of black autonomy, frequently became targets. In

Meridian, Mississippi, in 1871, some thirty blacks were murdered in cold blood, along with a white Republican judge. At Colfax, Louisiana, two years later, scores of black militiamen were killed after surrendering to armed whites intent on seizing control of the local government.

The Klan's purposes, however, extended far beyond party politics. Former slaves who had managed to obtain land were victimized, as well as those who had learned to read and write. The Klan, one white farmer commented, did "not like to see the Negro go ahead." Its aim was to restore white supremacy in all areas of Southern life—in government, race relations, and on the plantations.

Mississippi Klansman, 1871. (American Social History Project, Herbert Peck, Jr.)

Between 1868 and 1871, a wave of Klan violence swept over the South. State officials tried with varying degress of success to repress the Klan but, as violence persisted, Congress enacted the Ku Klux Klan Act in April 1871. The Act for the first time designated certain crimes committed by individuals as offenses punishable under federal law. It also authorized the use of federal marshals to suppress the Klan. In September 1871, federal marshals captured this Klansman, who reportedly turned state's evidence and revealed secrets, rituals, and signs of the organization.

Klansman on horseback, c. 1868 (Tennessee State Museum).

Members of the Ku Klux Klan disguised themselves in hooded robes while committing criminal acts against Southern blacks and their Republican allies. Hooded horses added another element of terror. This klansman holds a banner embellished with a dragon motif and the Latin motto referring to blacks: Quod Semper, Quod Ubique, Quod Abomnibus, *meaning "Because it always is, Because it is everywhere, Because it is abominable."*

The new Southern governments proved unable to restore order or suppress the Klan. Many sheriffs were too frightened to try to arrest those who committed acts of violence, and when they did, Klansmen—often the only witnesses—refused to testify against their compatriots. In a few states, including Arkansas and Texas, Republican governors used the state militia effectively

IF HE IS A UNION MAN OR A FREEDMAN.

'VERDICT' HANG THE D— YANKEE AND NIGGER

If He Is A Union Man or Freedman. Verdict, "Hang the D—— Yankee and Nigger"
engraving by Thomas Nast, Harper's Weekly, *March 23, 1867.*

The Ku Klux Klan sucessfully paralyzed Reconstruction governments in many localities by beating, shooting, and lynching an untold number of blacks and white Unionists.

against the Klan. Generally, however, the Reconstruction governments appealed to Washington for help.

Although some Northern Republicans opposed further intervention in the South, most agreed with Sen. John Sherman of Ohio, who affirmed that the "power of the nation" must "crush, as we once before have done, this organized civil war." In 1870 and 1871, Congress adopted three Enforcement Acts, outlawing terrorist societies and allowing the president to use the army against them. These laws continued the expansion of national authority during Reconstruction by defining certain crimes—those aimed at depriving citizens of their civil and political rights—as federal offenses rather than merely violations of state law. In 1871, President Grant authorized federal marshals, backed up by troops in some areas, to arrest hundreds of accused Klansmen. After a series of well-publicized trials, in which many of the organization's leaders were jailed, the Klan went out of existence. In 1872, for the first time since the Civil War, peace reigned in the former Confederacy.

Despite the Grant administration's effective response to Klan terrorism, the North's commitment to Reconstruction waned during the 1870s. Many Radical leaders, including Thaddeus Stevens, who died in 1868, had passed from the scene. Within the Republican party, their place was taken by politicians less committed to the ideal of equal rights for blacks. Many Northerners felt that the South should be able to solve its own problems without constant interference from Washington. The federal government had freed the slaves, made them citizens, given them the right to vote, and crushed the Ku Klux Klan. Now, blacks should rely on their own resources, not demand further assistance from the North.

In 1872, a group of Republicans, alienated by corruption within the Grant administration, bolted the party. Their ranks included some of the nation's most influential journalists, and a number of prominent Republican leaders, including Lyman Trumbull and other founders of the party. The Liberal Republicans, as they called themselves, claimed that the Civil War and Reconstruction had brought to power a new group of corrupt politicians, while men of talent and education like themselves had been pushed aside. They also believed that unrestrained democracy, in which "ignorant" voters such as the Irish immigrants of New York City could dominate politics in some locales, was responsible for such instances of corruption as the Tweed Ring. Governmental positions, they believed, should go to men who could pass demanding examinations, not to the political cronies of politicians, and that the propertyless and uneducated should have less of a say in government.

Democratic criticisms of Reconstruction found a receptive audience among the Liberals. As in the North, Liberals believed, the "best men" of the South had been excluded from power while "ignorant" voters controlled politics. The result was corruption and misgovernment. Government in the South should be returned to the region's "natural leaders."

In 1872, the Liberals nominated Horace Greeley, editor of the *New York Tribune,* to run against Grant. The Democrats endorsed Greeley, and the continuation of Reconstruction became a major issue in the campaign. Although the Liberals and Democrats pledged to uphold African-Americans' new constitu-

Colored Rule in a Reconstructed (?) State, *by Thomas Nast,*
Harper's Weekly, *March 14, 1874.*

Thomas Nast, a longtime proponent of black rights, expressed his discouragement with Reconstruction by depicting members of the South Carolina legislature arguing amongst themselves. Nast's caricature suggested that Reconstruction was a travesty of democracy and contrasted sharply with his earlier, more optimistic views.

tional rights, Greeley demanded a restoration of "local self-government in the South" and called upon Americans to "clasp hands across the bloody chasm" by putting the Civil War and Reconstruction behind them.

The Liberal attack on Reconstruction, which continued after Grant overwhelmingly won reelection, contributed to a resurgence of racism in the North. Journalist James S. Pike, a leading Greeley supporter, in 1874 published *The Prostrate State,* an influential account of a visit to South Carolina. In it, he depicted a state engulfed by political corruption and governmental extravagance,

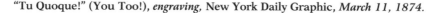

"Tu Quoque!" (You Too!), *engraving,* New York Daily Graphic, *March 11, 1874.*

An unknown artist responded to Thomas Nast's image of the South Carolina legislature (copied in the upper right corner) by lampooning the famous cartoonist. The cartoon carried the following caption: "Artistic Colored Gentleman—'I Wonder How Harper's Artist Likes To Be Offensively Caricatured Himself?' Second Colored Gentleman—'Golly, If Harper's Picture Is Nasty, Yours Is Nastier.'"

and under the control of "a mass of black barbarism." "Negro government," he insisted, was the cause of the South's problems; the solution was to see leading whites restored to political power. Pike's observations led even newspapers that had long supported Reconstruction to condemn black participation in Southern government. These same journals expressed their views visually as well. Increasingly, engravings depicting the former slaves sympathetically, as heroic Civil War veterans, upstanding citizens, or victims of violence, were replaced by caricatures presenting them as little more than unbridled animals.

Other factors also weakened Northern support for Reconstruction. In 1873, the country plunged into a severe economic depression. Distracted by the nation's economic problem, Republicans were in no mood to devote further attention to the South. Congress did enact one final piece of civil rights legislation, the Civil Rights Act of 1875, which outlawed racial discrimination in places of public accommodation. This was a tribute to Charles Sumner, who had devoted his career to promoting the principle of equality before the law, and who died in 1874.

Nonetheless, it was clear that the Northern public was retreating from Reconstruction. One reason Republicans adopted the Civil Rights Act was that Democrats, for the first time since before the Civil War, swept the elections of 1874 and would control the House of Representatives beginning in December 1875. Meanwhile, the Supreme Court began whittling away at the guarantees of black rights that Congress had adopted. In the *Slaughterhouse Cases* (1873), the court decreed that the Fourteenth Amendment had not altered traditional federalism; most of the rights of citizens remained under state control. Three years later, the Court, in *United States v. Cruikshank,* gutted the Enforcement Acts by throwing out convictions of some of those responsible for the Colfax Massacre. Henceforth, Southern Republicans, white and black, could expect little further help from Washington.

By the mid-1870s, Reconstruction was on the defensive. The depression dealt the South a severe economic blow, and further weakened the possibility that Republicans could create a revitalized Southern economy. Factionalism between blacks and whites and carpetbaggers and scalawags remained a serious problem among Southern Republicans. One by one, the South's Reconstruction governments were toppled.

In those states where Reconstruction survived, violence again reared its head, and this time, the Grant administration showed no desire to intervene. In contrast to the Klan's activities—conducted at night by disguised men—the violence of 1875 and 1876 took place in broad daylight, as if to flaunt Democrats' conviction that they had nothing to fear from Washington. In Mississippi, in 1875, white rifle clubs drilled in public, and Republicans were openly assaulted and murdered. At Clinton, African-Americans were shot "just the same as birds"—some thirty were killed, including teachers, church leaders, and local Republican organizers.

When Governor Adelbert Ames frantically appealed to the federal government for assistance, President Grant responded that the Northern public was "tired out" by Southern problems and would condemn any interference from

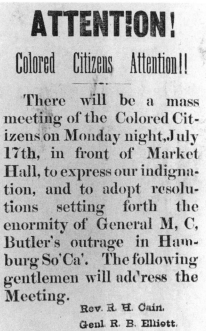

Attention! Colored Citizens Attention!, *broadside, 1876.*
(South Carolina Historical Society)

A notice for South Carolina's black citizenry to protest the Hamburg Massacre refers to Gen. Mathew C. Butler, the area's most prominent Democrat, who led hundreds of armed whites in an attack against the town's black militia in early July 1876. Among those listed to speak at the rally was Robert B. Elliott, noted black leader and former congressman from South Carolina.

Washington. On election day, armed Democrats destroyed ballot boxes and drove former slaves from the polls. The result was a Democratic landslide and the end of Reconstruction in Mississippi. "A revolution has taken place," wrote Ames, "and a race are disfranchised—they are to be returned to . . . an era of second slavery."

Similar events took place in South Carolina in 1876. Here, where blacks comprised 60 percent of the population, Democrats nominated for governor Wade Hampton, one of the state's most popular Confederate veterans.

WADE HAMPTON

Wade Hampton, c. 1876.
(Valentine Museum, Richmond, Virginia)

The governor who "redeemed" South Carolina from Republican rule, Wade Hampton (1818–1902) was born in Charleston, the son of a prominent member of the planter aristocracy. In the 1840s, his family began acquiring land in the Mississippi Delta, and in 1860 Hampton owned 900 slaves there.

During the Civil War, Hampton won fame as a Confederate cavalry commander. He emerged from the war as one of the state's most popular figures, and although he refused to be a candidate for governor in 1865, a write-in campaign on his behalf was only narrowly defeated.

Saddled with enormous debts, Hampton played little part in politics for most of Reconstruction. He did try to "direct the negro vote" in 1867, and when unsuccessful, denounced Reconstruction as unconstitutional and advocated removing the freedpeople from the state.

In 1876, Hampton became the Democratic candidate for governor. He pledged to expand the state's educational system and protect blacks against violence, but his supporters launched a campaign of intimidation that neutralized South Carolina's large Republican majority. Both parties claimed victory, and Hampton became governor as part of the Bargain of 1877.

As governor, Hampton favored a paternalistic policy toward the former slaves, and appointed a few blacks to minor positions. He was elected to the U.S. Senate in 1878, serving until 1891.

Of Course He Wants to Vote the Democratic Ticket,
Harper's Weekly, *October 21, 1876.*

In the 1876 campaign in South Carolina, Democrats launched a campaign of terror and violence in an attempt to wrest control of the state from the Republican party.

Hampton promised to respect the rights of all citizens of the state, but his supporters, inspired by Democratic tactics in Mississippi the previous year, launched a wave of intimidation, with rifle clubs disrupting Republican meetings, and freedmen being driven from their homes, assaulted, and sometimes murdered. Democrats intended to carry the election, one planter told a local black official, "if we have to wade in blood knee-deep."

Events in South Carolina directly affected the outcome of the presidential campaign of 1876. To succeed Grant, the Republicans nominated Gov. Rutherford B. Hayes of Ohio. His Democratic opponent was New York's governor, Samuel J. Tilden. By this time, only South Carolina, Florida, and Louisiana remained under Republican control. And as it turned out, the election was so

He Wants Change, Too, *by Thomas Nast,* **Harper's Weekly,** *October 28, 1876.*

Nast's cartoon, drawn in response to South Carolina's violent 1876 election campaign, depicts blacks as victims but also warns of the possibility of their taking up arms in self-defense. "The Boast of the Solid South" features quotes from several Southern Democratic newspapers proclaiming the right to use force against blacks in order to remove Reconstruction governments from power.

Campaign bandanas, printed cotton, 1876. (National Museum of American Life)

In the presidential campaign of 1876, Ohio's Republican governor, Rutherford B. Hayes, and his running mate, Judge William A. Wheeler of New York, defeated the Democratic ticket of Samuel J. Tilden, governor of New York, and Thomas S. Hendricks of Indiana. Hayes doubted the effectiveness of Northern intervention in Southern affairs while Tilden focused on issues of political corruption and economic depression. The Tilden-Hendricks bandana commemorates the nation's centennial by including a portrait of George Washington.

close that whoever captured these states—which both candidates claimed to have carried—would become the next president.

As in the winter of 1860–61, Americans again, sixteen years later, faced a political and constitutional crisis. There was anxious talk of civil war, but also intense negotiations involving leaders of both parties and self-appointed maneuverers representing Southern railroads anxious to receive federal aid. In January 1877, unable to resolve the crisis on its own, Congress appointed a fifteen-member Electoral Commission, composed of senators, representatives, and Supreme Court justices. Republicans enjoyed an 8 to 7 majority on the Commission, and to no one's surprise, the members decided that Hayes had carried the disputed Southern states and was elected.

Controlling the House of Representatives, Democrats could still obstruct Hayes's inauguration, but after secret discussions with representatives of the incoming president, they decided not to do so. This was the famous Bargain of 1877—Hayes would recognize Democratic control of the remaining Southern states, and Democrats would not block the certification of his election by Congress. Hayes became president, promised to end federal intervention in the South, and ordered United States troops, who had been guarding the state houses in South Carolina and Louisiana, to return to their barracks (not to leave the region entirely, as is widely believed). The Redeemers, as the Southern Democrats who overturned Republican rule called themselves, now ruled the entire South. Reconstruction had come to an end.

The collapse of Reconstruction deeply affected the future course of American development. In many parts of the South, the Republican party soon disappeared and the region long remained a bastion of one-party rule under the control of a reactionary elite who used the same violence and fraud that had helped defeat Reconstruction to stifle internal dissent. Despite its expanded authority over citizens' rights, the federal government stood by indifferently as the Southern states effectively nullified the Fourteenth and Fifteenth Amendments and, beginning in the 1890s, stripped African-Americans of the right to vote. Until then, blacks in some areas continued to hold public offices, but with Democrats firmly in command of state governments, black politicians found it extremely difficult to exercise authority on behalf of their constituents.

After the end of Reconstruction, Southern governments began to enact laws mandating racial segregation in schools, transportation, and public accommodations. In 1896, in *Plessy v. Ferguson,* the Supreme Court ruled that such segregation did not violate the Fourteenth Amendment's guarantee of equal protection before the law, so long as facilities for the two races were "separate but equal."

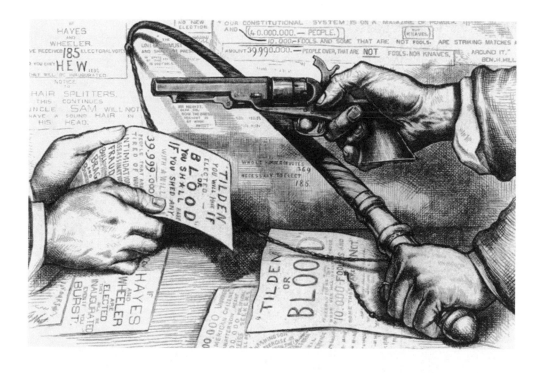

Tilden or Blood, *by Thomas Nast,* Harper's Weekly, *February 17, 1877.*

In the aftermath of the 1876 election, both candidates claimed victory. The disputed election threw the nation into a crisis, resolved by an independent commission, which decided the election in favor of Hayes. Nast's cartoon derided the Democrats' claims that bloodshed, and possibly a civil war, would result if Tilden did not become president.

In practice, however, facilities for blacks, whether schools, hospitals, or railroad cars, were markedly inferior to those for whites. By the turn of the century, Southern blacks found themselves enmeshed in a complex system of oppression, each of whose components—segregation, economic inequality, political disempowerment—reinforced the others. Those accused of crimes, or who sought to challenge the South's new racial system, faced a rising threat of violence. Between 1880 and 1968, nearly 3,500 African-Americans were lynched in the United States, the vast majority in the South.

Although the black institutions created or strengthened after the Civil War—the family, church, and schools—survived the end of Reconstruction, governments in the New South fell far behind the rest of the nation in meeting

Centennial, *lithograph by Ed. W. Welcke & Bro., New York, 1876.*
(Wadsworth Atheneum, Amistad Foundation)

As the nation celebrated the one-hundredth anniversary of the Declaration of Independence, it looked with optimistic pride upon its past and future. Although the imagery of Centennial *presented the Emancipation Proclamation as the culmination of the Declaration's promise, by 1876 American efforts to extend equal citizenship rights to black Americans had begun to wane.*

their public responsibilities. White Southerners suffered as well as black, as expenditures on education, health, and public welfare remained well below those in other states. New laws strengthened the hands of landlords in disputes with tenants, and state governments resolutely opposed the introduction of labor unions. Long into the twentieth century, the South would remain the nation's foremost economic problem, a region of low wages, stunted economic development, and widespread poverty. Millions of poor Southerners, black and white alike, felt their only hope for economic opportunity and social justice was to migrate to other parts of the country.

Not until the 1950s and 1960s would the nation again attempt to come to terms with the political and social agenda of Reconstruction.

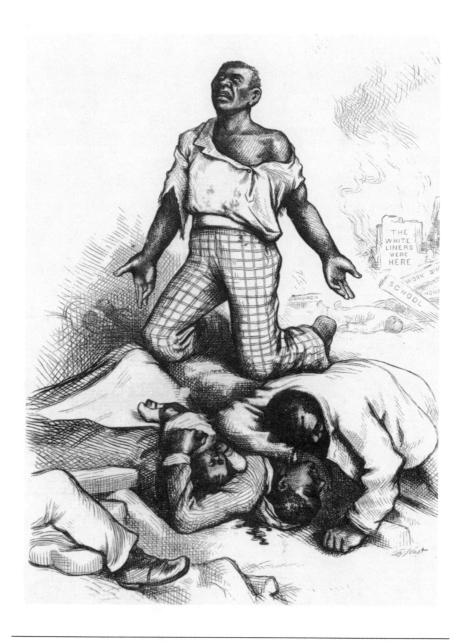

Is This a Republican Form of Government?, *by Thomas Nast,* Harper's Weekly, *September 2, 1876.* (National Museum of American History, Smithsonian Institution)

Thomas Nast, the nation's most prominent political cartoonist and a longtime proponent of civil rights, viewed the end of Reconstruction as a tragedy and questioned whether the nation was truly prepared to live up to its democratic creed by offering black citizens equality before the law and protection against violence.

FURTHER READING

The historical literature on Reconstruction is voluminous. This list offers a brief sampling, concentrating on the most important recent works. For a comprehensive history of the period and an extensive bibliography, see Eric Foner, *Reconstruction: America's Unfinished Revolution, 1863–1877* (New York, 1988), also available in abridged form as *A Short History of Reconstruction* (New York, 1990). Michael Perman, *Emancipation and Reconstruction, 1862–1879* (Arlington Heights, 1987) offers a brief, up-to-date survey of the era. Dorothy Sterling, ed., *The Trouble They Seen* (New York, 1976), and LaWanda and John H. Cox, *Reconstruction, the Negro, and the New South* (Columbia, 1973), are valuable collections of documents.

The traditional view of Reconstruction is reflected in William A. Dunning, *Reconstruction: Political and Economic 1865–1877* (New York, 1907); Claude G. Bowers, *The Tragic Era* (Cambridge, 1929); and E. Merton Coulter, *The South During Reconstruction 1865–1877* (Baton Rouge, 1947). W. E. B. DuBois, *Black Reconstruction in America* (New York, 1935), posed an exhaustive challenge to this interpretation. A generation later, Kenneth M. Stampp, *The Era of Reconstruction 1865–1877* (New York, 1965), and John Hope Franklin, *Reconstruction After the Civil War* (Chicago, 1960), summarized the revisionist critique.

The best accounts of the destruction of slavery and enrollment of black soldiers may be found in Ira Berlin, et al., eds., *Freedom: A Documentary History of Emancipation* (New York, 1982–). Two books by Herman Belz, *Reconstructing the Union: Theory and Practice During the Civil War* (Ithaca, 1969) and *Emancipation and Equal Rights* (New York, 1978), describe the evolution of wartime Reconstruction policy. For Lincoln's program, see LaWanda Cox, *Lincoln and Black Freedom: A Study in Presidential Leadership* (Columbia, 1981), and Peyton McCrary, *Abraham Lincoln and Reconstruction: The Louisiana Experiment* (Princeton, 1978). Willie Lee Rose, *Rehearsal for Reconstruction: The Port Royal Experiment* (Indianapolis, 1964), traces events on the Sea Islands. Other wartime "rehearsals" are chronicled in Louis S. Gerteis, *From Contraband to Freedman:*

Federal Policy Toward Southern Blacks, 1861–1865 (Westport, 1973), and Janet S. Hermann, *The Pursuit of a Dream* (New York, 1981).

Leon F. Litwack, *Been in the Storm So Long: The Aftermath of Slavery* (New York, 1979), vividly portrays blacks' responses to the end of slavery. The impact of emancipation on the black family is treated in Herbert G. Gutman, *The Black Family in Slavery and Freedom, 1750–1925* (New York, 1976), and Jacqueline Jones, *Labor of Love, Labor of Sorrow: Black Women, Work and the Family, from Slavery to the Present* (New York, 1985). For the rise of the black church, see Clarence E. Walker, *A Rock in a Weary Land: The African Methodist Episcopal Church During the Civil War and Reconstruction* (Baton Rouge, 1982), and Stephen W. Angell, *Bishop Henry McNeal Turner and African-American Religion in the South* (Knoxville, 1992). Robert C. Morris, *Reading, 'Riting, and Reconstruction: The Education of Freedmen in the South 1861–1870* (Chicago, 1981), traces the rise of schooling for blacks. Edward Magdol, *A Right to the Land: Essays on the Freedmen's Community* (Westport, 1977), explores the land issue, and Eric Foner, *Nothing But Freedom: Emancipation and Its Legacy* (Baton Rouge, 1983), places the land and labor questions in comparative perspective.

James L. Roark, *Masters Without Slaves: Southern Planters in the Civil War and Reconstruction* (New York, 1977), presents the response of slaveholders to emancipation. For the reactions of the Charles C. Jones, Jr., family, see Robert M. Myers, ed., *The Children of Pride* (New Haven, 1972). The war's impact on Southern yeomen is treated in Steven Hahn, *The Roots of Southern Populism: Yeoman Farmers and the Transformation of the Georgia Upcountry, 1850–1890* (New York, 1983). Catherine Clinton and Nina Silber, eds., *Divided Houses: Gender and the Civil War* (New York, 1992), suggests how the war affected the status of Southern women. For the rise of the idea of the Lost Cause, see Gaines M. Foster, *Ghosts of the Confederacy: Defeat, the Lost Cause, and the Emergence of the New South* (New York, 1987).

Numerous works address the transition from slave to free labor and the South's economic transformation. Among the most valuable are: Roger L. Ransom and Richard Sutch, *One Kind of Freedom: The Economic Consequences of Emancipation* (New York, 1977); Jonathan M. Wiener, *Social Origins of the New South: Alabama 1860–1885* (Baton Rouge, 1978); Ronald F. Davis, *Good and Faithful Labor: From Slavery to Sharecropping in the Natchez District, 1860–1890* (Westport, 1982); Steven V. Ash, *Middle Tennessee Society Transformed 1860–1870: War and Peace in the Upper South* (Baton Rouge, 1988); and Gerald D. Jaynes, *Branches Without Roots: Genesis of the Black Working Class in the American South 1862–1882* (New York, 1986). Accounts of the work of the

Freedmen's Bureau include William S. McFeely, *Yankee Stepfather: General O. O. Howard and the Freedmen* (New Haven, 1968); Donald G. Nieman, *To Set the Law in Motion: The Freedmen's Bureau and the Legal Rights of Blacks, 1865–1868* (Millwood, 1979); and Claude F. Oubre, *Forty Acres and a Mule: The Freedmen's Bureau and Black Landownership* (Baton Rouge, 1978).

The most recent assessment of Andrew Johnson's presidency may be found in Hans L. Trefousse, *Andrew Johnson* (New York, 1989). Eric L. McKitrick, *Andrew Johnson and Reconstruction* (Chicago, 1960), remains indispensable for understanding Johnson's personality and policies. The results of his Reconstruction policies are made clear in Dan T. Carter, *When the War Was Over: The Failure of Self-Reconstruction in the South, 1865–1867* (Baton Rouge, 1985). For white Southern attitudes see Michael Perman, *Reunion Without Compromise: The South and Reconstruction 1865–1868* (New York, 1973).

Hans L. Trefousse, *The Radical Republicans: Lincoln's Vanguard for Racial Justice* (New York, 1969), is the best history of this influential group. Several important works chronicle the breach between Johnson and Congress, among them W. R. Brock, *An American Crisis* (London, 1963); Michael Les Benedict, *A Compromise of Principle: Congressional Republicans and Reconstruction 1863–1869* (New York, 1974); and LaWanda Cox and John H. Cox, *Politics, Principle, and Prejudice 1865–1866* (New York, 1963). On civil rights legislation and the Fourteenth Amendment, see Robert Kaczorowski, *The Politics of Judicial Interpretation: The Federal Courts, Department of Justice, and Civil Rights, 1866–1876* (New York, 1985). Ellen C. DuBois, *Feminism and Suffrage: The Emergence of an Independent Women's Movement in America, 1848–1869* (Ithaca, 1978), explores feminists' response to the postwar amendments. For impeachment and the election of Grant, see Michael Les Benedict, *The Impeachment and Trial of Andrew Johnson* (New York, 1973), and Brooks D. Simpson, *Let Us Have Peace: Ulysses S. Grant and the Politics of War and Reconstruction* (Chapel Hill, 1992).

Michael W. Fitzgerald, *The Union League Movement in the Deep South: Politics and Agricultural Change During Reconstruction* (Baton Rouge, 1989), examines the political mobilization of the black community. Recent studies of black Reconstruction leaders include Okon E. Uya, *From Slavery to Public Service: Robert Smalls 1839–1915* (New York, 1971); Peggy Lamson, *The Glorious Failure: Black Congressman Robert Brown Elliott and the Reconstruction in South Carolina* (New York, 1973); James Haskins, *Pinckney Benton Stewart Pinchback* (New York, 1973); and the essays in Howard N. Rabinowitz, ed., *Southern Black Leaders of the Reconstruction Era* (Urbana, 1982). Among collective studies of black officeholders are Thomas Holt, *Black Over White: Negro Political Leadership in South*

Carolina During Reconstruction (Urbana, 1977); Charles Vincent, *Black Legislators in Louisiana During Reconstruction* (Baton Rouge, 1976); and Edmund L. Drago, *Black Politicians and Reconstruction in Georgia* (rev. ed.: Athens, 1992). Eric Foner, *Freedom's Lawmakers: A Directory of Black Officeholders During Reconstruction* (New York, 1993), contains biographical information on nearly 1,500 black officials.

Richard N. Current, *Those Terrible Carpetbaggers: A Reinterpretation* (New York, 1988), revises the image of Northerners who went to the South during Reconstruction. See also Otto H. Olsen, *Carpetbaggers' Crusade: The Life of Albion Winegar Tourgée* (Baltimore, 1965). On scalawags, see Sarah H. Wiggins, *The Scalawag in Alabama Politics, 1865–1881* (University, 1977); Gordon B. McKinney, *Southern Mountain Republicans: 1865–1900* (Chapel Hill, 1978); and Lillian A. Pereyra, *James Lusk Alcorn: Persistent Whig* (Baton Rouge, 1966).

Good introductions to Reconstruction in individual Southern states may be found in Otto H. Olsen, ed., *Reconstruction and Redemption in the South* (Baton Rouge, 1980). Among the best state studies are Jerrell H. Shofner, *Nor Is It Over Yet: Florida in the Era of Reconstruction, 1863–1877* (Gainesville, 1974); Joe Gray Taylor, *Louisiana Reconstructed, 1873–1877* (Baton Rouge, 1974); William C. Harris, *The Day of the Carpetbagger: Republican Reconstruction in Mississippi* (Baton Rouge, 1979); Carl Moneyhon, *Republicanism in Reconstruction Texas* (Austin, 1980); and Richard G. Lowe, *Republicans and Reconstruction in Virginia, 1856–70* (Charlottesville, 1991). An excellent account of Reconstruction at the local level may be found in W. McKee Evans, *Ballots and Fence Rails: Reconstruction on the Lower Cape Fear* (Chapel Hill, 1967). Works that concentrate on the black experience in individual states include Joe M. Richardson, *The Negro in the Reconstruction of Florida, 1865–1877* (Tallahassee, 1965), and Joel Williamson, *After Slavery: The Negro in South Carolina During Reconstruction, 1861–1877* (Chapel Hill, 1965).

Howard N. Rabinowitz, *Race Relations in the Urban South 1865–1890* (New York, 1978), and Roger A. Fischer, *The Segregation Struggle in New Orleans 1862–77* (Urbana, 1974), trace the evolution of race relations. Republican economic policy, and the problem of corruption, are examined in Mark W. Summers, *Railroads, Reconstruction, and the Gospel of Prosperity: Aid Under the Radical Republicans, 1865–1877* (Princeton, 1984). For the political opposition to Reconstruction, see Michael Perman, *The Road to Redemption: Southern Politics, 1869–1879* (Chapel Hill, 1984).

The most comprehensive history of the Ku Klux Klan is Allen W. Trelease, *White Terror: The Ku Klux Klan Conspiracy and Southern Reconstruction* (New York, 1971). See also George C. Rable, *But There Was No Peace: The Role of Violence in the Politics of Reconstruction* (Athens, 1984). William Gillette, *Retreat from Reconstruction 1869–1879* (Baton Rouge, 1979), traces the Grant administration's abandonment of Southern Republicans. Blanche B. Ames, ed., *Chronicles from the Nineteenth Century: Family Letters of Blanche Butler and Adelbert Ames* (Clinton, 1957), contains graphic descriptions of the violent Mississippi election of 1875. For the election of 1876 and Bargain of 1877, see Keith I. Polakoff, *The Politics of Inertia: The Election of 1876 and the End of Reconstruction* (Baton Rouge, 1973), and C. Vann Woodward, *Reunion and Reaction: The Compromise of 1877 and the End of Reconstruction* (Garden City, N.Y., 1956). Hampton M. Jarrell, *Wade Hampton and the Negro: The Road Not Taken* (Columbia, 1950), examines Hampton's policies.

 C. Vann Woodward, *Origins of the New South, 1877–1913* (Baton Rouge, 1951), remains the starting point for understanding the post-Reconstruction South, but see also two recent studies, Howard N. Rabinowitz, *The First New South, 1865–1920* (Arlington Heights, 1992), and Edward L. Ayers, *The Promise of the New South, 1877–1906* (New York, 1992). Two excellent recent studies examine the process of reunion and some of its costs: Stuart McConnell, *Glorious Contentment: The Grand Army of the Republic, 1865–1900* (Chapel Hill, 1992), and Nina Silber, *The Romance of Reunion: Northerners and the South, 1865–1900* (Chapel Hill, 1993). The diaspora of poor whites and blacks seeking opportunity outside the South, and some of its consequences for modern America, are explored in Jacqueline Jones, *The Dispossessed* (New York, 1992).

ACKNOWLEDGMENTS

America's Reconstruction: People and Politics After the Civil War is the result of collaborative efforts involving many people in the academic and museum worlds. First, we must thank the National Endowment for the Humanities for their generous support in developing this project. NEH funding allowed us to work with such notable scholars as Ira Berlin, Distinguished Professor of History, University of Maryland; Pete Daniel, curator, National Museum of American History, Smithsonian Institution; David R. Goldfield, Robert Lee Baily Professor of History, University of North Carolina at Charlotte; Howard N. Rabinowitz, professor of history, University of New Mexico; and Nina Silber, assistant professor, Department of History, Boston University. We must also express our deep appreciation to our colleagues at more than fifty archives, libraries, and museums, who made materials from this period available, shared their knowledge, and encouraged us in many ways. Without their efforts, this project would not have been possible and we are indebted to them.

Frank Jewell, Director of the Valentine Museum and project director, made our work possible by sponsoring and directing the project. Eryl Platzer, director of museum operations, served as project coordinator. Ms. Platzer's ability to orchestrate various aspects of the project and its personnel were critical to its realization. Susan P. Tillett, museum consultant, directed our efforts as we applied to the NEH for funds to implement the project. Jim Sims, exhibition designer, made the subject of Reconstruction accessible to the public without sacrificing scholarship. His imaginative design helped audiences understand the drama and relevance of this critical period of American history. Jane Webb Smith, curator of decorative arts and curatorial assistant for the exhibition, traveled thousands of miles to locate artifacts at dozens of repositories, coordinated loan requests, ordered photographs for the book and exhibition, and helped in countless other ways. Gregg D. Kimball, historian, provided advice on the content and format of the exhibition, while Karen Holt-Luetjen, director of public programs, developed gallery activities and a lecture series that creatively instructed the museum audience. Additional members of the Valentine staff who provided assistance include: Judy Lankford, who coordinated the grant proposals to the NEH; Cheryl Greenday, business office manager; Teresa Toane, supervisor of reference services; Amanda Macaulay, coordinator of the educational initiative; Michael McGrann, director of public relations; Anne Podlesak, registrar; Barbara C. Batson, assistant curator of collection; and Lili Church, registrarial assistant. In addition, we would like to thank Marie Tyler-McGraw, consultant; Nancy Growald Brooks, editor; Barbara C. Levy, public programs consultant; and Randi Korn and Associates, for evaluation and interpretive planning.

Several individuals at the Chicago Historical Society were instrumental to the success of the project. They include Douglas Greenberg, the Society's president and director; Ellsworth H. Brown, past president and director, and current president of the Carnegie Institute; Russell Lewis, assistant director for research and curatorial affairs; Margery Melgaard, vice-president of administration; and Robert C. Nauert, vice-president of finance. For providing us with materials from the Society's collections, we are grateful to Janice McNeill, librarian; Archie Motley, curator of archives and manuscripts; Susan Samek, associate curator of costumes; Larry Viskochil, curator, and Eileen Flanagan, assistant curator of prints and photographs. Sylvia Landsman, secretary; Nancy Buenger, textile conservator; Catherine Bruck and Walt Keener, curatorial assistants; and the Society's photographers, John Alderson and Jay Crawford, also deserve our thanks.

Finally, we extend our thanks to Kym S. Rice, museum consultant, and to Sarah Davis McBride, for helping us locate materials for the project that otherwise might not have been included.

INDEX